THE 5 *Marriage* Mandates

A Story About Biblical Principles to Help Anyone Overcome Any Marital Challenge

Vincent & Valerie Woodard

WHOLE ARMOR MEDIA

Cover & Interior Design:
Vincent Woodard for Whole Armor Media

We hope that you will enjoy this book from Whole Armor Media. We strive to provide high-quality, thought-provoking books and products that communicate biblical principles to your real needs and challenges.

For more information on other books and products that will help you with all your important relationships, go to 5marriagemandates.com or email support@couplespursuit.com.

To our three children, ChaVonne, Laquan, Kyra, And our grandson, Judah. Thank you all for loving us through the growing season.

DISCLAIMER

The Biblical principles discussed in this book (when applied consistently and intentionally) will help anyone overcome marital challenges. However, we do not encourage anyone to remain in an abusive environment.

If you are in an abusive relationship or fear your life is in danger, please take yourself and/or your children to safety. Call 911 for medical care or call 988 for the National Crisis Lifeline for non-medical emergencies.

ACKNOWLEDGMENTS

For your great love, encouragement, and prayers, we are grateful to each of you:

Bishop Lynwood E. Batts: Your prophetic vision of us as a "couple of example" during our wedding ceremony still guides us today.

Johnnie "Mac" and Rose Hall: True friends who stood by us in our darkest moments; your unwavering support was our lifeline.

Evangel Fellowship Men's Encounter: Your event sparked Vincent's transformation, setting the stage for this book.

Malcolm and Meagan Eatmon: Your video challenge encouraged us to launch Couples Pursuit Marriage Mastery.

Pastor Ernestine Vines: A mentor and friend, your wisdom and spiritual guidance have enriched our lives.

Dr. Dennis and Dr. Cynthia Parker: Our spiritual covering at Spirit of Truth Christian Center, your leadership has shaped our mission.

To our Lord and Savior for His gift of redemption and grace for reconciliation.

To our family, friends, and loved ones, your support sustains us.

To our readers, may "The 5 Marriage Mandates" inspire lasting love and joy in your marriages.

With heartfelt thanks, Vincent and Valerie Woodard

Contents

The Introduction   **7**

Marriage Mandate #1: Covenant   **10**

The Breaking Point   10

A Sacred Promise   16

Why Is Marriage So Important To God?   26

The Covenant Mandate: 33

Marriage Mandate #2: Commitment   **43**

Beyond The Wedding Day   43

The Commitment Mandate: 59

Marriage Mandate #3: Communication   **67**

How To Open The Lines: 67

The Art Of Listening   69

The Communication Mandate: 78

Marriage Mandate #4: Connection   **86**

The Heart Of Emotional Connection   86

Intimacy Beyond Physical Connection   96

The Connection Mandate: 103

Marriage Mandate #5: Calibration   **111**

Embracing Change   111

Establishing Boundaries   119

The Calibration Mandate: 125

Last Chapter: The Follow-Up   **132**

When One Journey Ends, A New One Begins   132

About The Authors   **136**

Notes: **138**

The Introduction

The evening sun painted the walls of Elaine and Dorian's living room with a golden hue. The room was silent, except for the ticking of the antique clock on the mantle. But the calmness was deceptive, a stark contrast to the tension that simmered between them.

Elaine sat on the edge of the elegant chaise lounge, her hands clasped tightly in her lap. Dorian was opposite her, his eyes focused on the blueprint spread on the coffee table, but his mind was elsewhere.

"Are we ever going to talk about it, Dorian?" Elaine finally broke the silence. Her voice was soft, laced with a desperation that Dorian couldn't ignore.

His gaze met hers. "Elaine, we've been over this."

"No, we haven't." Elaine's voice wavered. "We've danced around it but never really discussed it."

The room fell silent again, save for the relentless ticking of the clock.

"Dorian," she continued, her tone gaining some strength. "I want to start a family again. I still want children."

His jaw clenched, and he ran his hand over his head. "We discussed this babe... you know our careers don't allow us that luxury."

Elaine shook her head, frustration flashing in her eyes. "Dorian, that's just an excuse, and you know it. Pediatricians juggle careers and families. There are other couples with demanding careers who make it work. It's not as impossible as you think."

Dorian sighed, looking down at the blueprint again. But his focus wasn't on the detailed lines and legends—it was on the truth he'd never spoken and wasn't ready to share.

"Babe," Elaine pleaded, "please, talk to me. Why don't you want to start a family?"

His silence was his reply.

Elaine was drenched in anger, frustration, and sadness—but most of all, she felt an overwhelming sense of helplessness. She loved Dorian, but their inability to communicate had driven a wedge between them. This exchange left them both emotionally drained and more distanced than before. The deafening silence that filled their living room now billowed through the halls of their home. Silence, unspoken words, and unresolved issues increased the growing rift between them.

Elaine's eyes were fixed on Dorian. "What can I do?" she asked herself. Her heart ached as she realized they needed help bridging this gap. Dorian sighed deeply in desperation. He didn't know how to give his wife what she wanted because he wasn't sure if his marriage could survive it.

This is why a man leaves his father and mother and bonds with his wife, and they become one flesh. Both the man and his wife were naked, yet felt no shame.

Genesis 2:24-25

Marriage Mandate #1: *Covenant*
"This is why..."

THE BREAKING POINT

For the past three years, the tension between Dorian and Elaine began to build like the discomfort of an unwelcome guest with no plans of leaving anytime soon. Conversations that once flowed naturally and were filled with laughter and shared dreams were now a succession of accusations and misunderstandings that ended in cold silence.

In the eyes of friends and family, they were a golden couple. Elaine's passion for pediatrics and Dorian's unique vision as an architect were desirable. They enjoyed the benefits their lucrative careers had afforded them, but lately, their once bright and joyous home began to feel more like a silent battlefield. What once felt like a little scrape had grown into a gaping wound.

One rain-soaked Thursday, the tension came to a head. As the downpour battered the windowpanes, Dorian sat in his study, aimlessly flipping through a stack of blueprints. His gaze returned to an unfinished design, a dream home he had once promised to build for Elaine. Now, the incomplete plans felt like a painful reflection of their crumbling relationship.

Meanwhile, Elaine was in the living room, her medical journals untouched. Her mind returned to their last argument about starting a family, a subject they now mutually avoided. As the storm raged, Elaine found herself walking towards Dorian's study, a decision fueled by desperation. "Dorian, we need to talk," she said, her voice barely above a whisper.

Dorian looked up, his face etched with worry. The sight of his wife looking so defeated weighed heavily on him. "Elaine, I...," he began, but his voice trailed off. He didn't know what to say. They were both wearied by the weight of the void growing between them.

A flurry of thoughts coursed through Elaine's mind. How had they arrived at this point? To outsiders, they exemplified the perfect couple, but behind closed doors, she felt the intimacy fading year after year. "Should I bring up counseling again?" she wondered. Though she knew Dorian was hesitant about it, the idea had often crossed her mind.

Elaine remembered meeting Vincent and Valerie Woodard at a charity event last year. As founders of Couples Pursuit, the Woodards shared insights into their platform aimed at fortifying marriages. They emphasized the critical role of the five marriage mandates, which serve as the bedrock of Couples Pursuit.

During their discussion, they stressed that marriage is more than a contractual agreement but a lifetime bond between two people that must be nurtured, cultivated, and protected to thrive. Elaine agreed, but because she was confident things would turn around for her and Dorian, she didn't think much more of the encounter.

The Woodards went on to say that although there was no rulebook for marriage per se, they had discovered the principles and practices that rescued their dying relationship within the pages of the Bible. This idea was foreign to Elaine. She went to church from time to time as a child and had even been baptized, but she could not recall anything she'd heard about rules for marriage.

Elaine wanted to know more about Couples Pursuit. She found the website online and became even more intrigued by what she discovered. The Woodards' marriage was completely transformed after twelve years of turmoil and dysfunction.

They were on the verge of divorce until they took the focus off changing one another and concentrated on improving themselves. The process included self-reflection and individual counseling, but cultivating their relationship with God was the game-changer.

Testimonials from other couples were echoing the same sentiment. Though Elaine had no idea how Couples Pursuit could help her marriage, it was a lifeline she was willing to cling to.

Elaine looked intently at her husband. "Dorian, do you remember Vincent and Valerie Woodard, the guest presenters at the charity event we were invited to last year?" I want you to see what other couples are saying about them. There might be something to these marriage mandates, and I want us to try it. Elaine reached for her phone to show him the website she had pulled up.

As Dorian turned his attention to his wife, he was reaching into the recesses of his memory. He did remember them; he remembered the room, filled to the brim with couples. On stage stood Vincent and Valerie Woodard, baring their souls to a room full of relative strangers.

Vincent, a seemingly confident man, talked about his struggles as a husband and admitted to being a boy trapped in the disguise of a man, reeling under the pressure of frustrations he didn't know how to handle.

Valerie, a gentle and insightful woman, always tried to dig deeper to uncover the root of the frustration, which usually led to an argument.

On the other hand, Vincent was a master at avoidance, always choosing to ignore issues rather than confront them.

Vincent wasn't physically abusive, but his anger manifested in ways that were equally, if not more, damaging to the emotional health of his wife and family. Things would go from better to worse -again and again.

Over time, the strain became too much for Valerie. Vincent's frustrations and refusal to address the problems and emotional turmoil he was experiencing eventually led to them living separately in their own home. The discussions that followed were heartbreaking. Eventually, it all came to a head, and they began discussing dividing assets. Who would get what furniture, who would get the big screen TV, and how would they manage the mortgage? Most importantly, what did the future hold for their children?

Vincent shared with us an experience that changed his life - a Men's Encounter that he was invited to by his friend Mac. Throughout the weekend, the event featured worship, scripture reading, prayers, and encouragement from Christian men who had once been in similar situations.

"It is hard to heal from a pain you don't acknowledge even exists."

The men were encouraged to express to God their grievances, pains, and frustrations that they had buried inside but never shared openly. It is hard to heal from a pain you don't acknowledge even exists. Vincent bore his soul - confusion and frustration about his past, upbringing, and a father he never knew. He wondered why God would allow him to get married if it would end in divorce.

Vincent felt that God had abandoned him, but amidst his emotional upheaval, he experienced what he could only describe as God embracing him. It was a spiritual hug; a profound love and comfort enveloped him and began an inner healing.

He knew it was God's presence. At that moment, Vincent

finally understood what love was supposed to feel like.

That encounter became a turning point for Vincent. The more he learned about this God, the more he wanted to know. God is love... he had heard it before, but now he knew it for himself. As a result, he realized that he could not save his marriage unless he began to see her in the light of God's love. Then, he could learn to love his wife more as God intended. What if he shared his experiences with other men going through similar situations? It may also be possible to restore their marriages.

He was eager to share this God-kind-of-love with his wife and family - it would become his purpose and passion. Vincent decided then and there that he wouldn't lose his family, didn't want a divorce, and couldn't carry the burdens of life alone.

Vincent was changed forever. He surrendered everything to God and committed to be a better husband and father. After returning to his family, he made a promise to Valerie that he would be the man she needed, the man his family deserved. As part of his commitment, he promised to communicate openly and honestly to nurture their relationship so that it would never again be in danger of breaking down.

Dorian recalled how Vincent and Valerie admitted their unpreparedness when they first married and how they had drifted apart when faced with difficulties. They also shared how the pastor prophesied they would be a "couple-of-example" during their wedding ceremony.

Nearly twelve years later, that prophecy was beginning to unfold. And it all began with their renewed commitment to God and one another. Now, they were there on that stage, a beacon for others, sharing their gathered wisdom.

The 5 Marriage Mandates they'd discovered transitioned them from a place of pain and hopelessness to a place of reconciliation and profound love and understanding.

As he heard Elaine gently calling his attention to the Couples Pursuit website she'd pulled up on her phone, Dorian was drawn back to the present, his memories still resonating. Vincent was so vulnerable and transparent.

Dorian had never seen these characteristics exhibited in a man. He wanted to know more. What if Vincent could help him find his way back to his wife? He looked at Elaine, her hopeful eyes fixed on him. And with a deep breath, he nodded. "Alright, Elaine. Let's try."

Their words hung in the air, echoing their newfound determination to save their marriage. And while the storm continued to rage outside, inside, a warm glimmer of hope grew between them.

A SACRED PROMISE

Dorian and Elaine anxiously awaited their appointment. They arrived at Couples Pursuit's office on a crisp Tuesday evening; it was warm, serene, open, and welcoming.

Framed photographs graced the walls, capturing moments of joy, love, and shared experiences. Bookshelves were filled with volumes that reflected a deep understanding of human relationships and a strong belief in God's guiding principles.

Vincent greeted them with a warm smile. "We're grateful you remembered us and our chat from the charity event," he said, guiding them to a cozy seating area. Valerie initiated the discussion, her eyes reflecting a depth of compassion. "We wrote about the 5 Marriage Mandates because we know firsthand what it feels like to be burned out, frustrated, and hoping, praying, something would change in your relationship."

Vincent continued, "We understand the struggle of feeling like you're barely holding your family together. You're left wondering, 'How long can we survive like this, and are we even on the right path?'" A heavy silence filled the room as Elaine and Dorian exchanged glances. These words echoed their feelings, their frustrations, and their fears.

Their minds raced with wonder. Where is this elusive marriage handbook, and how can we get it? Is the guide to a happier, more fulfilling relationship within our reach? Is it even possible? Could this couple's wisdom, experience, and biblical principles help us heal the fractures in our marriage?

Outside, the sun was beginning to set, painting the sky in hues of red and gold. The warm light cast a gentle glow on a picture that hung on the wall - a painting of two hands clasped together, a perfect symbol of unity.

The couple exchanged nervous glances. They were not used to talking about their relationship with one another, let alone with strangers, but they were committed to taking this journey. They knew this was something they both needed.

"Marriage isn't just a contract; it's a covenant, a sacred promise."

"The first of the 5 Marriage Mandates we'll explore is Covenant," Vincent continued. "Marriage is more than just a contract; it's a covenant, a sacred promise. This change in perspective can profoundly impact how you navigate life moving forward."

A contract is a good thing, right? Dorian glanced at Elaine, feeling a little unsure. He had been thinking of their marriage as a 50/50 contract. But seeing it as a promise, a covenant, this perspective stirred something within him.

Valerie added, "It's about looking at each other not just as husband and wife but as partners on their way to becoming a single entity. It's not about erasing your individuality but cultivating the addition of "we."

Dorian and Elaine found themselves in a state of reflection. Dorian reached for Elaine's hand, mirroring the painting on the wall. It was a small step, but it felt significant. A faint smile tugged at Elaine's lips. She felt hope stirring in her heart for the first time in a long while.

SEEING MARRIAGE AS A SPIRITUAL BOND:

"Think back to your wedding day," Vincent began. His voice was calm and measured, a rock amidst the storm of Elaine and Dorian's turbulent emotions. "Do you remember the vows you exchanged? The promises you made to one another?"

Elaine and Dorian nodded in agreement. Of course, they remembered. How could they forget? That day was etched in their memories - full of joy, love, and promise. A day when they stood before friends, family, and God to declare their commitment to one another.

"You entered into a covenant that day," Vincent continued, "A promise that goes beyond a legal contract. A spiritual bond binds you together, with the purpose of you both becoming one."

"One," Valerie added, her voice gentle but firm. "Even when the road gets rough. Even when you disagree, are hurt, or feel like giving up. It means choosing each other, again and again, every day."

Vincent turned to a bookshelf behind him, pulling out a Bible. "Covenants are at the heart of this sacred book," he said, flipping through the gently worn pages. " The word covenant derives from the Old Testament, the Hebrew word "berith." Berith means "to cut; a cutting," with reference to the dividing of animals into two parts. One example of this reference to cutting is found in Genesis, chapter 15. God made a promise to Abram (later called Abraham) concerning his future and his lineage. Abram, having no children, questioned how this would come to pass. God answered by giving him the details of what would take place and then instructing Abram to prepare for the sacrifice that would seal the covenant of promise. This signified the sacredness and significance of the alliance being made".

God made covenants throughout history with his creation. Adamic Covenant: Made with Adam, it outlined the consequences of disobeying God in the Garden of Eden. (Genesis 3:16-19)

- **Noahic Covenant**: Made with Noah after the flood, promising never to destroy the earth again with a flood. (Genesis 9:8-17)

- **Abrahamic Covenant**: Made with Abraham, promising land, descendants, and blessings to his offspring, ultimately fulfilled through Jesus Christ. (Genesis 12:1-3, Genesis 15:18-21, and Genesis 17:1-14)

- **Mosaic Covenant**: Made with Moses and the Israelites at Mount Sinai, providing the Ten Commandments and the Law. (Exodus 19-24)

- **Davidic Covenant**: Made with King David, promising an everlasting kingdom and throne through his descendants, ultimately fulfilled in Jesus Christ. (2 Samuel 7:8-16)

- **New Covenant**: Prophesied in the Old Testament (Jeremiah 31:31-34), fulfilled by Jesus Christ, offering forgiveness of sins and a personal relationship with God through faith in Jesus' sacrifice. (Hebrews 8:6-13 and Luke 22:20)

Valerie added, "This is a great deal of information to digest, but you can learn more about this subject in your personal study time. We will be happy to share all the scriptures we referenced.

It is important to note that not all covenants involve the shedding of blood. Still, they all represent a solemn agreement or pact between parties and were central to the relationship between God and His people, establishing terms, promises, and obligations. But what makes marriage a covenant?

The New Covenant highlights Christ's relationship with the Church. The Book of Ephesians, specifically verses twenty-two through thirty-one, outlines the significance of this relationship:

- Wives are instructed to submit to their husbands as they do to the Lord, for the husband is the head of the wife, just as Christ is the head of the Church.

• Husbands are instructed to love their wives as Christ loved the Church and gave Himself for it. They are to cherish and nourish their wives as they do their own bodies, as Christ does for the Church.

• The passage emphasizes the unity between husband and wife, citing the creation story where a man leaves his parents to be joined with his wife, becoming one flesh.

• This relationship between husband and wife is described as a great mystery, symbolizing the relationship between Christ and the Church.

The New Covenant replaces the sacrifices and the shedding of the blood of animals with the redemptive work of Christ on the cross. He sacrificed once and for all. His blood also gives us access to God, the Father, and God, the Holy Spirit. This supernatural relationship was ordained by God, and marriage is His mystery. Along with the benefit of romantic love, companionship, sex, and procreation, He has given us the great privilege and responsibility to be a reflection to the world of His desire for love and fellowship with His creation.

"A spiritual bond binds you together, with the purpose of you both becoming one."

"Your marriage is among those sacred covenants," Valerie explained. "It's more than just an earthly agreement; it's a promise that echoes into eternity. In Christian theology, marriage is regarded as a sacred covenant ordained by God, wherein husband and wife commit to a lifelong partnership of love, faithfulness, and mutual support. While the concept of a blood covenant through consummation may not be emphasized in contemporary Christian teachings, the spiritual significance of marriage as a covenant relationship remains central.

Your love for each other and commitment to stay together through the highs and lows reflects God's unfailing love for His people. With a covenant, God is in the midst of your marriage. He is the foundation it is built on and the glue that holds it together. It was Him who created you and designed you for one another. It only makes sense that He would be central to its purpose and essential to its success."

This was a perspective they had never considered before. Dorian felt a strange mixture of conviction and comfort. He had been viewing their relationship through a lens of conditional love, the kind that wavered and changed with circumstances.

But what Vincent and Valerie described was a steadfast and unchanging love. Elaine was silent but thoughtful.

The realization that their vows weren't just words but a promise, a covenant, carried a weight and a warmth that seemed to fill the empty spaces between them.

"God made covenants with His people, binding promises that He always keeps."

THE BIBLICAL DEPTHS OF COVENANT

Vincent leaned back in his chair, his fingertips gently pressed together. He seemed to be considering his words carefully before he spoke. "It's important for you to grasp the principle of covenant fully. Honoring the significance of covenant is vital to the success of your marriage."

He opened the Bible he had pulled from the shelf, flipping the pages until he found the passage he sought. "Genesis 9:11-17," he read out loud. Noah was faithful in building the ark even though he had never seen rain.

Despite the ridicule he faced for obeying God's instructions, he did not waver. God spared him and his family. This scripture exemplifies an unbreakable covenant, made entirely by God's grace."

Elaine and Dorian listened. These were familiar stories heard in Sunday sermons and Bible studies.

Yet, in this context, they took on a whole new meaning. Their wedding vows weren't just promises but a reflection of God's enduring faithfulness to His people.

"It's more than just an earthly agreement; it's a promise that echoes into eternity."

"Covenants," Vincent said, closing the Bible and looking at them, "are not just agreements written on paper. They are living relationships that involve commitment, obedience, and blessing.

God initiates them, carried out by His grace, and are the cornerstone of His redemptive plan for us. And that," he pointed towards them, "includes your marriage."

A silence settled in the room. It was a lot to take in. Dorian could feel the weight of the words settling on him. Their marriage was more than a contract. It was meant to be a covenant, a living, breathing relationship that could only survive if grounded in Biblical principles.

Elaine felt the same. Her heart fluttered with a mixture of fear and hope. Their marriage and struggles had more significance than they had ever realized.

"There is hope for you," Valerie broke the silence, her voice a soft yet confident whisper. "It sounds like you are just beginning to realize the true meaning of your covenant. Now, we will give you some tools that will aid you in keeping it alive. It might not be easy, but nothing that matters ever is."

Imagine how difficult it must have been for Noah to stay the course. All those who opposed and made fun of him were lost forever, but Noah and his family were saved because he trusted and obeyed God. We still marvel at the miracle of the rainbow today, a sign of God's covenant promise to never flood the earth again.

WHY IS MARRIAGE SO IMPORTANT TO GOD?

Vincent began, echoing the day's warmth. "The first reference to marriage is found in Genesis 2:24." "This passage is a beautiful picture of the sacredness of marriage and the covenant formed therein."

He quoted the scripture, "'This is why a man leaves his father and mother and bonds with his wife, and they become one flesh.'" He let the words hang in the air for a moment before continuing. "This single verse paints a picture of a man leaving his family to create a new one with his wife.

It highlights the husband's responsibility to put his wife first, making her his primary source of companionship, support, and intimacy."

Dorian glanced at Elaine. His eyes were soft, something Elaine hadn't seen in a while. The idea of becoming one and creating something new together appealed to him. She felt a strange mix of comfort and unease. While the concept seemed right, it seemed so far removed from their daily lives.

Dorian's head shifted slightly, eyes meeting Vincent's. He seemed poised to voice a thought, then hesitated. Vincent caught the subtle cue. "Something on your mind, Dorian?"

After gathering his thoughts, Dorian asked, "I think I understand that God honors our marriage covenant, but why is marriage so important to God?"

Vincent and Valerie exchanged glances before Valerie began, "Well, marriage is important to God for several reasons."

Vincent nodded, "Marriage was God's idea, a foundation for all humanity. Remember Genesis? A man leaves his parents and joins with his wife."

Valerie added, "Marriage also reflects God's Love. Think about it: God loves us even more than a husband loves his wife. Ephesians 5:25 says it beautifully."

"Husbands, love your wives, just as Christ loved the church and gave Himself up for her,"

"Right," Vincent continued, "And it's a metaphor for Christ and the Church. The relationship between Jesus and the Church is a marital bond."

Valerie smiled, "Marriage also promotes holiness and growth. It's where we guide each other towards faith and grow spiritually."

Vincent leaned in, "And let's remember, through marriage, we experience deep connections, just as God planned from the beginning. Even though both the man and his wife were naked, they were not ashamed about it.

Valerie picked up where Vincent left off and said, "Marriage offers the best environment for raising children. Within this bond, your children and everyone in your household get love and stability."

Vincent continued, "And as we discussed, marriage is a covenant. It's more than just a contract; it's a promise made with God at the center."

"If we don't have a right relationship with God, we'll inevitably have a wrong relationship with our wife."

Vincent leaned forward, locking eyes with Dorian. "Put simply, marriage is God's demonstration of how Jesus is tied to the Church. As men, we strive to love our wives as Christ loved the Church.

But here's the catch: we're not Jesus. It's a high standard, and while we might not always meet it, our wives understand and respect our efforts."

He paused briefly, letting the weight of his words sink in. "A man can only continue to give love to his wife as he gets from God. If we don't have a right relationship with God, we'll inevitably have a wrong relationship with our wife."

"But it's not just about leaving and cleaving," Valerie said. "They shall become 'one flesh.' This represents not just physical unity but also a deep spiritual connection. Being one meant sharing everything: joys, sorrows, triumphs, failures, dreams, and fears."

Vincent added thoughtfully, "Remember, marriage begins when two people learn to trust God and become one. If you do, you will enter a new phase of your relationship, a kind of genesis."

There was something deeply profound about this thought. It meant mutual support, shared responsibility, and joint decision-making. It was a lot to consider, but it made sense.

Dorian and Elaine were listening attentively. They contemplated whether they ever clearly understood the concept of marriage. Their thoughts were being transformed.

"God himself sealed the covenant between Adam and Eve," Vincent added. "He is the one who joins the two in marriage, and He is the one who sustains their covenant. God makes the promise, and the couple makes the commitment.

Elaine and Dorian sat quietly, processing the depth of what was shared. Their marriage, they realized, was more than sharing names and a host of responsibilities. It was a pledge not just to each other but to God.

They had entered into a covenant. This was far more important than the proposal, the ring, the venue, the reception, the guest list, or the honeymoon.

The road ahead was undoubtedly challenging. It would require change and, most importantly, a willingness to place their relationship above everything else.

Elaine and Dorian felt a glimmer of hope as they sat with the weight of this revelation settling over them. They were not alone in this. They had each other, and they had God.

Elaine turned to Dorian, her voice soft but laden with hope. "Dorian, do you think we can start over? To create our new beginning?"

Looking into her eyes, Dorian felt a sense of determination stir. "Maybe that's exactly what we need," he replied thoughtfully. "A fresh start. Our own Genesis."

THE VIDEO

Later that evening, Dorian and Elaine found themselves seated on their couch, the flickering screen of their laptop illuminating the dimmed room. Their homework assignment was to watch a video from Vincent and Valerie's YouTube channel – 10 Key Foundations of a Kingdom Marriage.

Elaine was not surprised to hear that most people get married mainly to be happy and feel loved, but they were astonished to hear that those reasons are not the purpose of marriage but rather a benefit.

Love and happiness are desirable and expected; you should love the person you marry, but romantic love does not sustain a couple. Elaine wanted to know more about this topic and could not wait until their next session.

Another topic discussed in the video was prayer. The necessity of prayer, individually and as a couple, is vital to the success of a marriage. Vincent and Valerie shared how the power of prayer was a key factor in their reconciliation. They also shared how prayer can still be effective even when only one spouse is open to change.

Elaine and Dorian exchanged a glance. They had prayed before, individually, but never together outside of church, and never for each other. The idea was new, and yet it felt right.

"Pray for your spouse," Valerie encouraged. "Not as a means of manipulation, but as a means of intercession. Remember, you are one, so you want to pray for your spouse to be whole in every area of their life, especially those with weaknesses or flaws. It can transform lives."

They continued, discussing the importance of the roles within a marriage. "The husband's role," Vincent explained, "is compared to Christ's love for the church. He should lead with love and humility, protecting and providing for his wife."

"And the wife," Valerie said, "is to receive this love with grace, humility, and respect for her husband."

It was a profound thought. Their roles had less to do with

who did the cooking and cleaning or paid the bills and more with the spiritual depth and purpose discussed in the fifth chapter of Ephesians—marriage God's way was an illustration of the ultimate love story between Christ and His church.

As the video concluded, Vincent and Valerie prayed for their viewers, their voices sincere and comforting. "We pray that God guides you in your marriages and relationships, that you uphold your vows and seek godly counsel when needed."

They encouraged their viewers to reflect on their marriages, remember their vows, and share their reflections with their spouses or trusted friends.

Elaine turned to Dorian, her heart pounding. "Should we do it?" she asked. "Do you want to pray together?"

Dorian was quiet for a moment. Then, with a slight nod, he reached for her hand. "Yes," he said, his voice barely above a whisper. "Let's pray."

And so, they prayed together for the first time in a long time. It was awkward and beautiful, but it began their shared journey toward embracing their marriage as a covenant.

After they finished praying, the couple sat in their living room, no laptops, no phones, no videos playing in the background, just the soft glow of their table lamp.

Dorian picked up a picture frame from their bookshelf. It was a photo from their wedding day, both radiant and joyful.

"Honoring the significance of covenant is vital to the success of your marriage."

"We made a covenant, Elaine," he said quietly, his eyes still on the photo. "I knew I was making a promise, but this is more than I ever understood. I let our problems and disagreements make me lose sight of how important you are to me." Elaine reached over, gently covering his hand with hers. "I was so focused on getting what I wanted that I lost sight of the fact that we are one. And being one requires more than I have been giving".

Her voice was barely above a whisper, and the words welled up in her like water and gently flowed down her cheeks. Elaine added, maybe we didn't fully understand before, but we're learning now, and that's what matters."

In the heart of their home, amidst the stillness of the night, Dorian and Elaine took a moment to appreciate the gravity and the beauty of the covenant they had made to each other, the promise that was so carefully created for them to embody and to enjoy.

THE COVENANT MANDATE:

I acknowledge and accept that marriage is more than a contract; it's a covenant. It is a gift and a calling. I will honor marriage as the sacred institution God designed it to be.

Study Guide

next page ☞

THE 5 Marriage Mandates

Covenant

Study Guide

Introduction to the Study Guide:

Whether you are facilitating a group session or studying alone or with your spouse or future spouse, this study guide is designed to help you delve deeper into the principles discussed in each chapter. The study will last 5 weeks and should stimulate great discussion among the participants.

Here are some simple instructions:

For Group Leaders:

1. **Prepare in Advance**: Review the chapter and the study guide questions beforehand. Familiarize yourself with the key concepts and takeaways.

2. **Create a Welcoming Environment**: Encourage open and respectful discussion in a safe space. Make sure everyone feels comfortable sharing their thoughts and experiences.

3. **Facilitate Discussion**: Use the provided questions to guide the conversation. Encourage participants to share their personal insights and how the concepts apply to their relationships.

4. **Keep the Focus on God and Growth**: Remind the group that the goal is to grow together in understanding and applying the marriage mandates. Keep the discussions constructive and centered on the principles of faith.

For Individual or Spousal Study:

1. **Read and Reflect**: Start by reading the chapter and reflecting on the key concepts. Take notes on how the principles resonate with you.

2. **Discuss with Your Spouse**: If you are studying with your spouse, set aside time to discuss the questions. Be honest and open in your discussions.

3. **Personal Application**: Think about how you can apply the concepts to your daily life. Use the action plans and prayer suggestions to integrate the mandates into your marriage.

4. **Pray Together**: Dedicate time to pray, asking God for guidance and strength in your relationship.

General Tips:

- **Be Consistent**: Set a regular schedule for your study sessions, whether weekly or bi-weekly.

- **Stay Committed**: Commit to completing the study guide and encourage each other to stay engaged.

- **Seek Support if Needed**: If you encounter challenges or have questions about the study guide, don't hesitate to contact us at support@couplespursuit.com.

Study Guide
Marriage Mandate #1: *Covenant*

Chapter Summary:

Chapter One explores the importance of the Covenant as the cornerstone of marriage. This spiritual bond exceeds the legal terminology of a contractual agreement and recognizes God as its creator. This sacred promise between a man and a woman is designed to be a lifelong journey. In a covenant, a husband and wife grow through the love and support of one another that is deeply rooted in the principles of their faith.

Key Concepts and Takeaways:

- **Understanding Covenant:** Recognizing covenant as a prerequisite to marriage highlights its sacredness and the importance of commitment.

- **Spiritual Bond:** Covenant Marriage is a spiritual commitment with God at the center.

- **Shared Growth:** Covenant Marriage requires another's spiritual, emotional, and physical support to grow and thrive.

Discussion Questions:

1. How does the concept of 'Covenant' change or challenge Elaine and Dorian's relationship?
- Explore how their perception of marriage solely as a contractual agreement affects their relationship.

2. What does the term 'covenant' mean to you in the context of marriage?
- How might viewing your marriage as a covenant alter your approach to challenges and growth?

3. How can you incorporate the idea of a covenant into your daily married life?
- Have you discussed Covenant Marriage with your spouse? If so, brainstorm ways to integrate the concept into your daily interactions and decisions.

4. In what ways does understanding your marriage as a covenant with God change your perspective about persevering through difficult times?
- Reflect on how seeking God's presence in your marriage can provide strength and guidance during challenging times.

5. How might the view of marriage as a covenant impact how couples resolve conflicts?
- Discuss how viewing your marriage as a covenant could influence your approach to disagreements and the process of problem-solving.

THE COVENANT ACTION PLAN:
Weekly Spiritual Bonding Activity

- **Scripture Study:** Set aside time every week to study a Bible passage related to marriage. Discuss its relevance and what you both can learn from it.

- **Prayer Time:** Dedicate a specified time each day, even if it's just five minutes, to pray together, specifically asking God for guidance as a couple.

- **Refocus on God:** Remember that God is the architect of marriage and should be at its core. Be intentional about centering your marriage on God and His love. Seek His guidance and assistance in renewing your covenant.

- **Recommit to your vows:** Reaffirm your commitment to your spouse and God daily.

- **Reconcile:** If your covenant has been broken, seek to rebuild trust between yourself and your spouse. This will involve honest communication, forgiveness, and reconciliation. It may also require mentorship or counseling.

- **Re-read the Marriage Mandate on *Covenant*:** What does this mandate mean to you?

Weekly Prayer:

Dear God,

We want to thank you for the incredible gift of marriage and the beautiful covenant it represents. As we journey through this life together, we ask for your help in strengthening our bond through your Word and prayer. You are the creator of our love story, and we seek your guidance to keep our relationship centered on your love and purpose. Please give us the strength to honor our vows daily and remain true to them. When we face challenges, hurt, or broken trust, lead us toward open and honest communication, grant us the grace to forgive, and bring healing to our hearts. Bless our relationship, Lord, and keep us united in your love.

In Jesus' name, we pray.

Amen.

Reflection Notes:

This is why ***a man leaves his father and mother and bonds with his wife***, and they become one flesh. Both the man and his wife were naked, yet felt no shame.

Genesis 2:24-25

Marriage Mandate #2: *Commitment*

"...a man leaves his father and mother..."

BEYOND THE WEDDING DAY

In their next session, Vincent and Valerie decided to delve deeper into the second Marriage Mandate, 'Commitment.' They focused on the powerful vows often recited at wedding ceremonies and wanted to unpack their profound implications.

Vincent began, "The principle at the heart of this mandate is the commitment to stand by each other through thick and thin, to love, honor, and cherish each other for the entirety of your lives."

"In a marriage, one of the most difficult things to overcome is a broken heart caused by one or both spouses not being committed."

He paused for effect, then continued, "In a marriage, one of the most difficult things to overcome is a broken heart caused by one or both spouses not being committed. Many enter marriage with unrealistic expectations, believing they will never face heartache."

As he spoke, Dorian and Elaine shared a look. Elaine had always envisioned a perfect marriage - no fights, no heartbreak. Was that where she had gone wrong?

Valerie said, "We're not suggesting that you should become accustomed to heartbreak nor accept it as the norm. However, some enter marriage thinking their hearts will always remain intact, only to realize later that marriage can and does have its trials. We never anticipate stormy days, yet our marriage vows are stated in a way that helps prepare us for them in one simple phrase..." for better or for worse."

A silent agreement passed between Dorian and Elaine. They had indeed ignored that there may be '"for better or for worse" days' in their relationship.

"'For better or for worse' is there to prepare you for potential hardships."

Vincent then brought up a startling statistic, "The National Institutes of Health conducted a study on divorce, and they found that at least 75% of individuals indicated that the most common major contributing factor to divorce was lack of commitment. Of the couples in which at least one spouse mentioned commitment as a problem, 70.6% represented couples where both agreed that lack of commitment was a major reason for divorce."

Valerie leaned forward, looking intently at Elaine and Dorian. She said:

"Remember your wedding vows - 'for better or worse.' Why is 'for worse' included? To prepare you for potential hardships. 'For richer or poorer' - why mention 'poorer'? To ready you for financial challenges. 'In sickness and in health' - why include 'sickness'? To brace you for times of illness."

There will be difficult times, periods of sickness, and times when you wish you had more resources. But the question is, will you remain committed through these trials? Will you remove the thought of 'divorce' from your mind when adversity strikes? Anyone can commit during the sunny days, but it takes a dedicated person to remain committed during the stormy ones."

Their words reverberated within Elaine and Dorian. They sat quietly, mulling over the profound concepts.

HOW TO HOLD ON, NO MATTER WHAT

A covenant is not simply made; it is cut. If there is no blood, there is no covenant. God instituted marriage. He formed Adam from the dust of the ground, cut open his side, took a rib, and created Eve. Blood was shed as a demonstration of this covenant.

"Choosing to commit represents a spiritual testament of a sacrificial, permanent relationship."

A covenant that represents a spiritual testament of a sacrificial, permanent relationship. It demonstrates to your spouse that your commitment to each other is till death do you part. It's not just a fleeting promise, but a lifelong vow."

This hit Elaine and Dorian hard. They had never really discussed commitment in this depth before. They had always loved each other but wondered if they'd been truly committed, especially during the tough times.

Vincent looked on his bookshelf to retrieve Emerson Eggerichs' book, 'Love and Respect: The Love She Most Desires; The Respect He Desperately Needs,' to delve deeper into commitment.

"There's a chapter in this book," Vincent began, "titled 'Loyalty—She Needs to Know You're Committed.' The title alone conveys the importance of reassuring your spouse of your love and commitment.

Imagine a scenario where a wife asks her husband if he still loves her and will be there for her even when they grow old, even in the face of adversity. How should the husband respond?"

Dorian shifted uncomfortably, "Well, the correct response would be... yes," Dorian answered.

Vincent continued, "That's correct. The right response is to reassure with conviction, and this, in turn, strengthens the bond between you two."

The book talks about how one of the most important things a man needs in a relationship with a woman is respect and love. It isn't that the wife does not want respect from her husband, nor does the husband not want love from his wife. However, respect is generally the number one priority for a man, and love is the number one priority for a woman. A husband feels loved when his wife respects him, and a wife feels respected when she feels loved by her husband.

When couples go through trials and are not committed to the relationship, two things happen: the husband withholds his love, which leads to the wife withholding her respect.

Vincent leaned in, his eyes meeting Dorian's. "This world is filled with temptations that crouch at the door of our heart, waiting to gain entrance. Whatever the distraction is, be it physical, mental, emotional, sexual, spiritual, or financial, we must always consider how our daily decisions can affect our future. These are the areas where commitment is truly tested."

He gestured to the wedding bands on Dorian and Elaine's fingers. "These rings symbolize more than just your vows. They embody your love and loyalty, a constant reminder of your devotion to each other."

Vincent added, "As husbands, we must be open, understanding, and loyal. We should never mention divorce, even in a joking manner. It shakes the very foundation of the security that a marriage provides."

He shared a scripture, Malachi 2:13-14:

13 Another thing you do: You flood the Lord's altar with tears. You weep and wail because he no longer looks with favor on your offerings or accepts them with pleasure from your hands. 14 You ask, "Why?" It is because the Lord is the witness between you and the wife of your youth. You have been unfaithful to her, though she is your partner, the wife of your marriage covenant.

"This scripture emphasizes marriage's sanctity in God's eyes, especially regarding how we treat our wives. "Our marriages are not just about us. They're also about our covenant with God. This spiritual alignment deepens our commitment, allowing us to stay on what Eggerichs calls 'The Energizing Cycle", which is a cycle that triggers and fuels itself. The cycle begins when a man shows his wife love or when she shows him respect.

Finally, Vincent concluded, In essence, the longevity and health of a marriage rely on the continual reassurance of love and commitment."

BUILDING A COMMITTED RELATIONSHIP

After much intense discussion and reflection, the Marriage Mandate session on Commitment drew to a close. As seasoned navigators in the rough seas of marital disputes, Vincent and Valerie sensed a shift in the room. The silence that hovered was not empty but pregnant with realizations.

Elaine sat quietly, her mind whirling with the insights gained. She had always been committed to Dorian. She was ready to weather any storm, to make any sacrifice. But a gnawing doubt had begun to eat at her conviction.

Across from her, Dorian looked distant, lost in thought. He grappled with the profound implications of the session. The enormity of commitment was daunting. He even questioned his commitment level, wondering if a lack of commitment was the cause of his marriage's breakdown. As they sat there in silence, their thoughts drifting yet intertwined, Elaine's heart was heavy with an unspoken question. As the seconds ticked away, her anxiety intensified. Finally, she voiced her fear in her thoughts, "I know I am committed, but is Dorian?"

The question hung in the air, a ponderous thought that would cast a long shadow on their journey ahead. It was a question that hinted at deeper issues, secrets yet to be unveiled, a heaviness that pressed down upon the very foundation of their relationship. It was a weight that threatened to crush them. It was inevitable that their pursuit of a healthier, stronger bond would bring them face-to-face with their individual and collective struggles.

With that, they left the room, their minds abuzz with thoughts and questions. The session had ended, but the journey was far from over.

It was only the beginning of a transformation that would demand the best from Elaine and Dorian - their unyielding commitment to each other and their marriage.

THE CONFESSION

After the session with Vincent and Valerie, Elaine and Dorian arrived home, both deep in thought. The house was quiet, amplifying the sound of their synchronized footsteps as they moved into their living room.

The silence was broken only by the dull hum of their living room lights; Elaine patiently waited for Dorian to release the burden he had carried for far too long. She studied her husband as he avoided her gaze, a man usually so confident now sinking under a wave of emotion pulling him under. She knew the session had brought something to the surface, a secret eating away at their relationship. After a moment of bracing himself, he finally spoke.

Elaine, there's something I've been keeping from you.

Dorian was silent momentarily, the weight of the impending confession heavy in the air. He looked away, his gaze focusing on a distant point as though he was gathering his strength from the abstract canvas of their shared history. His hands shook slightly, revealing the fear that was welling inside.

The silence stretched, filling the room with an uneasy tension. Elaine watched him, her heart pounding in her chest.

She could see the internal battle within him, the silent war that threatened to tear him apart. And it frightened her.

"Elaine..." Dorian finally began, his voice catching on her name. It was barely a whisper, the words seemingly caught in the lump in his throat. His hands clenched and unclenched, a physical manifestation of his inner turmoil.

He took a deep breath, attempting to draw strength from the air around him. "Elaine, there's something I need to tell you, "He said, his voice steadier this time. His tone filled her heart with dread. She wanted to shout, "What is it!" but fear clenched her jaws.

"It's... It's about my addiction," he finally confessed, his voice barely raised above the synchronized pounding of their hearts. The words echoed through their home like a whaling siren.

Elaine felt her world pause. An addiction? His confession hung in the air, pregnant with meaning and consequence. "What sort of addiction, Dorian?" she asked, her voice trembling, afraid of the answer.

Dorian swallowed hard, his throat dry and eyes glassy. "Pills, Elaine. I'm addicted to pills.

Pain shot through Elaine's heart as she took in his confession. But the worst was yet to come. Dorian took another deep breath; each word he spoke next weighed heavy with guilt.

"And... I've been using your credentials to get them. I used your prescription pad to get more pain pills," he added reluctantly, his gaze falling away from her again.

The admission hit Elaine like a punch in the gut. She sat back, her mind racing, feeling like the floor had been ripped from under her. How could she not know what was happening right under her nose? How bad was it, and what potential damage could this cause? What about her career and the reputation she had worked so hard to establish? These thoughts soon gave way to the sinking feeling of the reality of this betrayal by the man she loved so deeply.

She had to fight back tears as she spoke, her voice strangled with emotion.

"Dorian... how could you?" she whispered, a fragile mix of hurt, confusion, and anger.

Dorian's gaze fell to the floor, unable to meet Elaine's piercing eyes. He felt a knot in his throat as he struggled to find the words that might begin to explain the chaos he had brought into their lives. "I don't know...," he started, his voice barely above a whisper, "I never intended for any of this to happen."

He paused, collecting his scattered thoughts. "It started with the stress at work," he continued, his voice gaining strength yet laced with a deep sense of remorse. "I was drowning in it, and I began to drink more than usual. But that... that just made me feel worse, more depressed."

Elaine's expression softened slightly, but her eyes still held a glimmer of unresolved pain. She remained silent, prompting him to continue.

"Then, I thought smoking weed would help ease the stress, but it only made me paranoid. And then the back injury at work happened." Dorian's hands trembled slightly as he recounted the events. "The doctor prescribed opioids for the pain. They... they numbed more than just the physical pain, Elaine. They numbed everything, the stress, the pressure... and for a while, I felt relief."

He looked up at Elaine now, his eyes wet with unshed tears. "But when the prescription ran out, and the doctor wouldn't prescribe anymore, I..." he trailed off, unable to finish the sentence.

Elaine's heart raced as she listened, a painful realization dawning on her. "But why, Dorian? You used my prescription pad? Why wouldn't you just tell me? Why wouldn't you let me try to help you?"

Dorian's eyes were filled with a mixture of shame and desperation. "I couldn't stop, Elaine. The addiction, it... it took over. I wanted to stop, but I couldn't." His voice cracked under the weight of her sobering questions.

Still trying to piece together the puzzle, Elaine suddenly had a thought that chilled her to the bone. "Dorian, is it because I lost our baby?" Her voice was a fragile whisper, loaded with fear and vulnerability.

Elaine stared at Dorian, searching his face for the

desperately needed truth. There was a rumbling of emotions in her heart.

Dorian said nothing. He looked at her, his eyes pleading for understanding and forgiveness. But Elaine was far from forgiving. The betrayal felt raw, like a wound freshly opened.

She let the silence stretch, her mind racing as she tried to process the magnitude of Dorian's actions and the repercussions it could have on their lives. The trust in their relationship felt shattered, and her faith in him was severely shaken.

Yet, amid the tidal wave of her emotions, Elaine remembered Vincent and Valerie's teachings. The Marriage Mandates, especially about Commitment. She recalled their words, the awareness that commitment was about weathering the storm together and sticking by each other through the highs and the lows, but she wasn't expecting this.

She looked at Dorian, a man she had pledged to love and cherish, now broken and vulnerable. Her heart ached at the sight of him, a potent mix of love, betrayal, anger, and fear coursing through her veins.

Elaine sat silently for a moment, her mind numbed by the shock. The weight of Dorian's confession pressed upon her, a crushing, tangible force that stole her breath away. Tears welled up in her eyes as she processed the enormity of the revelation, each salty droplet marking a silent testament to her pain.

She thought of the trust she'd placed in her husband and her confidence in his character, and her heart crumbled with the realization of his deceit. The depth of his betrayal stung, her soul weeping for the man she'd thought she knew and for the countless moments of joy now tarnished by his actions.

At the same time, fear gripped her. She was terrified about the road ahead and the battle they would need to fight. She knew the path to recovery would be long and arduous, filled with trials and tribulations she could hardly begin to imagine.

Anger flared within her. She felt heat welling up in her cheeks and the muscles clenching in her jaw. She was furious at Dorian for deceiving her, risking their relationship, and endangering her career. She was angry with herself for not seeing the signs or being there for him. For a moment, she felt small.

"She tried to quell the whirlwind within her. It wasn't easy, the emotions demanding to be felt"

Still, beneath it all, there was love. A fierce, protective love that seemed to radiate from her very being. Despite the storm of emotions raging within her, despite the betrayal and the fear, she loved Dorian. And she understood, at that moment, 'in sickness and in health' was rising to test her commitment. She knew that she would need the benefit of everything she had just learned about covenant and commitment to survive this.

With a deep breath, she tried to quell the whirlwind within her. It wasn't easy; the emotions were demanding to be felt, and each one was vying for attention. But she felt a surge of determination.

Taking a deep breath, she reached out to Dorian, taking his trembling hands in hers, "I'm not going to lie, Dorian, this hurts me, it hurts like... and I don't know how we are going to deal with this, but I'm committed," she said, her voice firm despite the blinding tears streaming down her face.

At that moment, a profound realization dawned on Dorian. Witnessing the strength and resolve in Elaine's eyes, he was experiencing the true depth of commitment. He was embarrassed, hurt, and frustrated, yes, but more than anything, he was devastated by the pain he had caused her. Then, Dorian made a silent vow to himself - he would never knowingly and willingly inflict such hurt on Elaine again.

Tears, sober and full of regret, cascaded down his cheeks as he looked into her eyes. "I'm so sorry, Babe," he whispered, his voice choked with emotion. "I am so deeply sorry." Heavy with the weight of his newfound commitment, his words filled the space between them.

THE CALL

It would be a full week before Dorian and Elaine had another session with the Woodards.

Elaine felt desperation tugging at her heart. All the what-ifs and whys were swimming around in her head. She wanted things to work out but was also trying to figure out how this could affect her life and career. She requested an emergency virtual meeting, an option that Vincent and Valerie allow for circumstances like this.

Elaine and Dorian sat on separate chairs in their home to meet with Vincent and Valerie the next day. This time, they met with them via the computer screen in their home office. The room was silent momentarily as Elaine shared Dorian's secret. His addiction. His betrayal.

Valerie looked at them with compassion, but Vincent broke the silence. "Dorian," he began, his voice calm yet stern. "The first step to healing is acknowledging your actions and the pain they've caused. You've done that, which is good, but there is a long way to go. No matter how this addiction began, you will have to get to the root of why it became an option for you so that you can eliminate the possibility of it continuing."

"However," Valerie interjected, "while we are here to guide you through the principles of a healthy, Christ-centered marriage, we must acknowledge our limitations. We are not addiction counselors. We recommend seeking professional assistance to address this specific challenge."

Vincent nodded in agreement, "This is not to say we can't support you in other vital ways – one of which includes recommendations for addiction recovery specialists in your area. You may choose whomever you like, but we want you to have options rooted in biblical principles to supplement the healing you have begun here with us.

Overcoming such a challenge requires a spirit, soul, and body approach. Biblical principles direct us toward living a Spirit-filled life. In other words, we filter the activity of our soul (our mind, will, emotion, conscience, and intellect) through the lens of the Word of God guided by the Holy Spirit. The better we become at this, the less we surrender our bodies to sin, ultimately separating us from God."

Think of it this way: the body will follow the part of you that you feed the most. Galatians 5:16 - I say then: Walk in the Spirit, and you shall not fulfill the lust of the flesh.

Valerie interjected, "Please let us know when you have chosen an addiction recovery program. Elaine, you, too, will need support as Dorian recovers from pill abuse. Addiction affects not only the one who is addicted but potentially everyone attached to them, specifically spouses, family, friends, and co-workers. Elaine, we applaud your willingness to forgive and support Dorian through this process.

Still, you will also benefit from the assistance of these programs. The news of Dorian's addiction is fresh, but the effects and consequences can become overwhelming.

Staying connected to someone who understands this process is paramount to getting to the other side of addiction together."

THE COMMITMENT MANDATE:

I acknowledge and accept that commitment is one of the cornerstones of a successful and healthy relationship. Without it, a marriage won't survive.

Study Guide
next page ☞

THE 5 *Marriage* Mandates

Study Guide

Study Guide

Marriage Mandate #2: *Commitment*

Chapter Summary:

The second chapter of "The 5 Marriage Mandates" shifts to the crucial commitment aspect in marriage. Commitment goes beyond just staying together; it's about actively choosing your spouse every day, in good times and bad. The chapter highlights the importance of understanding it and touches upon how commitment is tested and the need to maintain it despite external and internal pressures.

Key Concepts and Takeaways:

- **Depth of Commitment:** Understanding commitment is an ongoing, active choice, not just a passive state of being together.

- **Facing Challenges Together:** Recognizing that commitment means standing by each other through life's ups and downs.

- **Upholding Vows:** Remembering and living by the promises made during the wedding, especially 'for better or for worse.'

Discussion Questions:

1. How do Dorian and Elaine struggle with commitment in their marriage?
- Observe the moments of tension and avoidance in their interactions, particularly around difficult subjects like family planning, etc.

2. How do you define commitment in your marriage?
- Share your views on what commitment means in your relationship, including how it's similar or different from societal norms.

3. Can you recall when your commitment was tested and how you handled it?
- Reflect on past challenges and discuss how you and your spouse managed to stay committed to each other.

4. What role do your wedding vows play in your everyday life?
- Discuss how the promises made during your wedding are reflected in your daily interactions and decisions as a couple.

5. In what ways can you strengthen your commitment to each other?
- Brainstorm ideas and actions that could help deepen the commitment in your marriage.

THE COMMITMENT ACTION PLAN:
Vow Renewal: How can we recommit to one another?

- **Reflect:** Revisit your marriage vows. What did you promise each other? What did you promise God? Are you upholding those promises?

- **Recommit:** Consider hosting a small vow renewal ceremony. This doesn't have to be elaborate but can be an intimate moment between the two of you, reaffirming your commitment.

- **Reevaluate the importance and value of commitment.** Reaffirm your commitment to each other and the vows you've made. Take a moment to reflect on what those vows meant to you then and what they mean now.

- **Reaffirm your relationship.** Make time for each other, even when you're busy. Talk about your feelings, needs, wants, and desires. Commit to prioritizing your relationship.

- **Renew your faith** in God's ability to strengthen and guide you as you pursue a covenant marriage. Pray together and read the Bible together.

- **Re-read the Marriage Mandate on Commitment:** What does this mandate mean to you?

Weekly Prayer:

Heavenly Father,
As we seek to renew and reaffirm our commitment, we ask for Your wisdom and guidance. Help us cherish and remember our vows to each other and You. Let us find joy and meaning in revisiting these promises, understanding their significance more each day. Guide us to prioritize our relationship, making time for each other amidst life's busyness. Strengthen our bond through Your love, and help us to continually renew our faith in You. May our marriage be a testament to the power of commitment and Your unending grace.

In Jesus' name, Amen.

Reflection Notes:

This is why a man leaves his father and mother *and bonds with his wife,* and they become one flesh. Both the man and his wife were naked, yet felt no shame.

Genesis 2:24-25

Marriage Mandate #3: *Communication*
"...and bonds with his wife"

HOW TO OPEN THE LINES:

"Developing healthy communication is vital to the survival of any relationship," Vincent began. You must be honest about your behavior, needs, and feelings. You must also be aware that the expression of both verbal and nonverbal communication plays a vital role in the success of your relationship. A listener/viewer receives mixed signals when what is said and done do not align".

> *"Communication is the lifeblood of a relationship."*

Valerie added, "Communication is the lifeblood of a relationship. You must be both honest and kind to one another. Ephesians 4:15 reminds us, 'Speak the truth in love, growing in every way more and more like Christ.' Being truthful with yourselves and each other is essential."

Vincent then introduced the concept of the 'Hierarchy of Needs', as developed by American psychologist Abraham Maslow. "This theory proposes that we have a series of needs, starting with the most basic and progressing to the most advanced. However, we've modified it into 'Understanding the Basic Needs of Your Spouse,' inspired by Maslow's work, yet backed by Biblical principles."

Vincent concluded, "Remember, understanding these basic needs is not just crucial; it is essential to the healing process. Your challenge now is to navigate through this tumultuous period, using these principles to rebuild and fortify your marriage."

"The most basic need in a relationship, especially for women, is security. That's why this hurts so much for Elaine", Vincent said intently to Dorian. "Her security has been violated, and it's up to you to strengthen it. "Physical needs, such as food, water, shelter, and rest, are the next level of the hierarchy."

The room was silent as Elaine nodded, tears welling in her eyes. Vincent then reached for a Bible on the table next to him and started reading, "Isaiah 41:10:

'Fear not, for I am with you; be not dismayed, for I am your God; I will strengthen you, I will help you, I will uphold you with my righteous right hand.'"

"The love and belonging in your marriage have also been shaken, Dorian," Valerie said. "This is another level of the hierarchy you need to work on. The Bible teaches us in 1 John 4:7-8: 'Beloved, let us love one another, for love is from God, and whoever loves has been born of God and knows God.

Anyone who does not love does not know God because God is love.'"

Vincent continued, "Next, there's respect and recognition. You have broken Elaine's trust, Dorian, and that's something you need to earn back. 'Do nothing from rivalry or conceit, but in humility count others more significant than yourselves' - Philippians 2:3."

"Finally, the highest level of the hierarchy is purpose, which you must find again, Dorian. Ephesians 2:10 states:

'For we are his workmanship, created in Christ Jesus for good works, which God prepared beforehand, that we should walk in them.'

And Dorian," Valerie added softly, "addiction is not your purpose. Remember, as you continue your journey to recovery, you must discover the "why" behind the "what"; otherwise, you could find yourself repeating the same behaviors or substituting one form of addiction for another."

The room was quiet again as Dorian nodded, tears streaming down his face. Elaine reached out to take his hand, a gesture of support and commitment.

THE ART OF LISTENING

Vincent and Valerie stood up, their message clear. "Dorian, only by understanding these basic needs and the

Biblical principles they are based upon can you start to heal and show your commitment to Elaine and your marriage. Elaine, remember you, too, have to heal from the effects of this addiction. Your willingness to do so will aid your husband in his recovery. You are in this together."

They left Elaine and Dorian alone with their thoughts, the path to healing and rebuilding their marriage laid out before them. They understood the journey would be long and hard, but they were committed to weathering the storm together.

DEEPER DIVE INTO COMMUNICATION

As Vincent and Valerie reentered the room, they found Elaine and Dorian, their faces dried from tears and carrying an air of determined resolution. Seeing their readiness, they knew it was the right time to share some crucial tools to help them navigate their storm.

Vincent started the discussion, "Elaine, Dorian, we now tackle the third mandate for a successful marriage - Communication. Honest, clear conversation is the key even when the subject matter is challenging."

Valerie chimed in, "And remember, communication is a two-way street. It's not just about talking but also about listening. What we say, why, and how we say it can either strengthen the bond or cause friction."

Vincent explained the role of communication in marriage.

"Many couples believe they communicate well but often skim the surface. Misunderstandings can brew in these shallow waters, escalating into conflicts. Hence, effective communication is paramount."

Introducing the significance of prayer in their formula, Valerie added, "Prayer is a mighty tool for improving communication. It can provide wisdom and guidance, especially during times of hardship. So never underestimate the power of prayer in your relationship."

NAVIGATING FEELINGS TOGETHER

Valerie then brought up the critical aspect of emotions in communication. "Emotions are indicators, not instructions. They can illuminate our feelings but are not meant to dictate our reactions. Therefore, learning how to express our feelings appropriately is a crucial skill to master. Take a moment to think about a time when you may have responded emotionally. If given the opportunity, would you change your response?"

Elaine interjected with a hint of frustration, "But what if every time we try to address something difficult, it just turns into an endless loop of conflict? It's like we're on this merry-go-round where Dorian either shuts down, tries to shut me down, or we end up in a blame game."

Dorian chimed in, equally troubled. "And I get frustrated because we're just circling, each trying to explain what the other person did wrong. It feels like we're stuck and not getting anywhere."

Vincent nodded, understanding the depth of their struggle. "This is where the 'STOP' method comes into play. It's a framework designed to guide you through emotionally charged conflicts thoughtfully. Let me explain each step."

1. **Stop:** "The first step is to pause before reacting impulsively. This pause prevents you from saying or doing something you might regret."

2. **Think:** "Use this time to reflect on what triggered you. What are you trying to communicate, and what's the outcome you're hoping for?"

3. **Observe:** "Notice your emotional and physical reactions. Are you angry? Is your heart rate up? This step is about becoming self-aware and empathetic about how your spouse is experiencing you."

4. **Proceed:** "After assessing the situation, decide how best to proceed. This could be through calm discussion, taking a break, or even adopting a different approach."

Vincent concluded, "Following these steps creates a gap between what triggers you and how you respond. This gap is crucial—it's where you find the choice and control over your reactions."

Elaine and Dorian absorbed the information, each recognizing the potential impact of this method in breaking their cycle of conflict.

"Emotions are indicators, not instructions."

Vincent then shared their devised communication plan. "To help couples discuss emotions, we have identified three categories of communication - Proactive, Personal, and Intimate. When employed properly, these can fortify your relationship."

Vincent continued to explain Proactive Communication. "We are often reactive in relationships. We wait until conflicts arise and then rush to resolve them.

This is where Proactive Communication comes in. It's about having forward-thinking conversations to anticipate potential issues and disagreements.

Consider setting aside specific times throughout the year for proactive conversations.

Focus on areas in your relationship that could use reinforcement or potential issues that might lead to disagreements."

Valerie interjected, "And always approach these discussions with prayerful hearts. Asking for godly wisdom can help you see the bigger picture in your relationship.

It's like choosing between 40 hours of solution-oriented dialogue or 40 weeks of conflict over the same issue. Or between 40 days of Proactive Communication and 40 years of a lukewarm marriage."

Continuing the discussion, Vincent introduced the second type of communication - Personal Communication. "This is about fostering a daily routine of talking about anything and everything.

Whether it's about your day, feelings, children, or ongoing projects, the continuous flow of conversation keeps the connection alive. Aim for at least 30 minutes each day.

A helpful tip: minimize digital distractions. Put away your phones and mute the TV to concentrate on each other truly."

"Intimate Communication goes beyond the physical aspect; it's about creating a warm and loving environment."

Valerie chimed in with the third and final type, Intimate Communication. "Intimacy goes beyond the physical aspect. It's about taking a few minutes each day to express affection both verbally and physically.

It's about creating a warm and loving environment, whether whispering sweet nothings, expressing your love, or just holding hands."

In conclusion, Vincent said, "Think of your relationship as a well-maintained vehicle. It needs regular maintenance, the right fuel, and careful handling.

Proactive, Personal, and Intimate Communications are the maintenance, fuel, and handling tools. Use them wisely, and your relationship will run smoothly on the road of love, respect, and understanding."

With these strategies, Vincent and Valerie were confident that Elaine and Dorian could navigate their storm and nurture their relationship toward recovery.

BUILDING EMOTIONAL INTIMACY

Elaine and Dorian shared a long look, their hands instinctively finding each other as Vincent and Valerie finished laying out their roadmap.

Their hearts fluttered, a mix of hope and apprehension beating in their chests. This was it - the beginning of their long journey towards healing.

A distinct sense of hope arose within Elaine. It was like seeing the promise of sunrise after an eclipse. They had a beacon that promised brighter days.

She clutched Dorian's hand, her grip a silent vow to be proactive, engage in daily personal talks, and create intimate moments.

Meanwhile, Dorian felt a knot of anxiousness in his stomach. The road ahead was fraught with potential pitfalls and harsh truths that must be faced.

But there was also a sense of relief. The weight of the unknown was slowly lifting, replaced with a plan of action, a strategy. They were no longer lost at sea. They had a compass now, and they were in this together.

They both knew that the path toward healing would be challenging. There would be moments of triumph, joy, despair, and frustration.

Yet, there was an undercurrent of gratitude in their hearts - gratitude for their knowledge and support system in Vincent and Valerie.

As they rose from their seats, their shoulders slightly less heavy, their steps a tad more confident, they knew one thing for sure - the journey would be challenging, but they were prepared to weather the storm together.

The session with Vincent and Valerie breathed new life into their perspective of their relationship. They now more than ever understood the importance of their covenant – a commitment to each other and the higher power that bound them together.

They were no longer merely a couple caught in a storm; they were no longer two halves of a whole. They were determined to be two whole and complete individuals, anchored by the covenant that makes them one.

Recommitment stirred within their hearts. This wasn't merely about survival but the growth and flourishing of their love. They had tools and strategies to pave their path with understanding and empathy.

Proactive communication, they knew, would be their lifeline, pulling them out of the reactive patterns that had trapped them for so long.

Personal communication is the threads that weave their days together, allowing them to share, listen, and understand. And then, there was intimate communication - the essence of their closeness - that promised to fan the spark of their relationship into a warming flame.

A newfound confidence started to replace the initial fear. Yes, the path was filled with obstacles, but they were amassing the tools to endure the journey.

They now had strategies to break down the walls between them. They were building their faith in God, their marriage, and each other; this was a new shared strength. Confidence in the principles they had begun to discover spurred them forward, hand in hand, ready to face the challenges ahead.

THE COMMUNICATION MANDATE:

I acknowledge and accept that I am responsible for communicating openly and honestly with maturity, integrity, and respect. I will honor my spouse and others by listening to hear and understand.

Study Guide

next page ☞

THE **5** *Marriage* **Mandates**

Study Guide

Marriage Mandate #3: *Communication*

Chapter Summary:

This critical chapter of "The 5 Marriage Mandates " focuses on Communication. It emphasizes the importance of honest, open, and respectful dialogue between spouses. The chapter delves into various aspects of communication, encompassing verbal and non-verbal forms of expression, and underscores the significance of acknowledging and attending to each other's emotional needs.

Key Concepts and Takeaways:

1. **Foster Trust and Understanding:** Prioritize transparency in communication to build trust and promote understanding.

2. **Practice Active Listening:** Actively listen and seek to comprehend each other's viewpoints in all conversations.

3. **Master Non-Verbal Communication:** Learn how to effectively convey messages through body language, tone, and actions.

4. **Prevent Miscommunications:** Implement strategies to prevent misunderstandings and avoid making assumptions during discussions.

Discussion Questions:

1. Can you identify moments in the story where Dorian and Elaine fail at effective communication?
- What communication strategies could they have applied to alter the outcome of these situations?

2. How do you balance expressing your emotions while respecting your spouse's feelings?
  - Reflect on how you convey your feelings in ways that do not cause your spouse to feel disrespected, dishonored, humiliated, or ashamed.

3. Can you recall a situation where poor communication led to a misunderstanding?
  - Reflect on if and how you resolved the misunderstanding and discuss what you learned.

4. How do you use non-verbal communication, and how does it impact your communication?
  - Share how actions, facial expressions, or body language can convey emotion, intent, and aggression.

5. What strategies do you find most effective in avoiding misunderstandings?
  - Brainstorm approaches to prevent miscommunications and share ideas to avoid them in the future.

THE COMMUNICATION ACTION PLAN:
How can we effectively communicate?

- **Be honest and open and kind.** Express your thoughts, feelings, and needs thoughtfully, considering how your words may impact your spouse, even during challenging moments.

- **Listen actively.** When your spouse is talking to you, listen to understand. This means paying attention to their words, body language, and tone of voice. It also means being aware of your own.

- **Be respectful.** If you disagree, express your thoughts and opinions without being dismissive of theirs. Differing viewpoints don't necessarily make one position superior to the other.

- **Avoid aggression.** Avoiding harmful tactics such as name-calling, insults, or shouting is crucial, as resorting to these behaviors can escalate conflicts and harm relationships.

- **Remain Positive:** Remember that the objective is reconciliation and mutual understanding. Prioritize finding solutions over assigning blame or insisting on being right.

- **Re-read the Marriage Mandate on Communication.** What does this mandate mean to you?

Weekly Prayer:

Heavenly Father,

As we seek to renew and reaffirm our commitment to our marriage, we ask for Your wisdom and guidance. Help us cherish and remember our vows to each other and to You. Let us find joy and meaning in revisiting these promises, understanding their significance more each day. Guide us to prioritize our relationship, making time for each other amidst life's busyness. Strengthen our bond through Your love, and help us to continuously renew our faith in You. May our marriage be a testament to the power of commitment and Your unending grace.

In Jesus' name, Amen.

Reflection Notes:

This is why a man leaves his father and mother and bonds with his wife, ***and they become one flesh.*** Both the man and his wife were naked, yet felt no shame.

Genesis 2:24-25

Marriage Mandate #4: *Connection*

"...and they become one flesh..."

THE HEART OF EMOTIONAL CONNECTION

As Elaine and Dorian took refuge inside Vincent and Valerie's office, she wondered how they got here.

Their story had sometimes been different. Once upon a time, a much younger Elaine and Dorian had embarked on a journey of togetherness, wrapped in the invincibility of love and youth.

Their wedding day, a snapshot of pure happiness, was a testament to their dreams and aspirations. However, as the nuances of life often dictate, even the most vivid of pictures may conceal the traces of a painstakingly detailed sketch.

Embedded in the annals of their shared history was a memory, at once triumphant and painful. The memory of Elaine, her body burgeoning with a life she had created with Dorian, her countenance radiating the unique glow of expectant motherhood.

Then, there was Dorian, his pride shining through his otherwise reserved demeanor, eagerly awaiting the day he would hold his flesh and blood.

Their joy was infectious, their home a sanctuary of love and anticipation. However, a cruel twist of fate robbed them of their joy, replacing it with a searing void. The life that had begun to form within Elaine was extinguished abruptly, pulling the rug from under their feet.

Elaine was left grappling with a profound loss that dimmed the light in her eyes.

On the other hand, Dorian was stripped of more than the prospect of fatherhood. He lost a fragment of his soul that sought solace in the dark abyss of pill addiction.

The after-effects of their loss were devastating. Their once vibrant home now echoed with deafening silence. Once filled with laughter and dreams, their conversations now reeked of unvoiced accusations and misunderstood intentions. The palpable tension was a constant reminder of the joy that had once been.

UNDERSTANDING THE ROOTS OF DISCONNECTION

Elaine still found herself wondering, was the loss of their unborn baby the trigger for Dorian's descent into addiction? Was her grief the catalyst for the chilling transformation of their home? The thought gnawed at her from the inside, amplifying her sense of guilt and despair.

How she wished they had discovered the Marriage Mandates earlier. The guidance may have equipped them with the skills to wade through the murky waters of grief, to weather the storm that threatened to dismantle their relationship. It may have given them the tools to heal, reconnect, and rekindle the love that once illuminated their lives.

After an eternity of agonizing introspection, the sessions with Vincent and Valerie became a lifeline for Elaine and Dorian, a space where they could unpack their challenges and fears, a sanctuary where their marriage could heal and strengthen. The road to healing is often paved with feelings of being overwhelmed but also anticipation and today's topic was no different.

EMBRACING THE STRUGGLE

The couple sat across from Vincent and Valerie, their countenances reflecting exhaustion and a newfound determination.

During the previous session, they discussed probable triggers for Dorian's addiction and the role that honest, transparent communication would play in helping them reconcile and recover.

They were willing to do the work and hear all the Woodards had to share, but the emotional toll it took was evident. Yet, they had emerged, holding hands tightly, symbolizing their renewed commitment to face the challenges together.

"Let's start with a quick recap," Valerie began, her soft, compassionate voice filling the room. "Our last mandate talked about the importance of effective communication, remember? You must have had some pretty intense conversations since then. How do you feel?"

Elaine glanced at Dorian, who gave her a small, encouraging smile. "It was tough," she admitted, "It's still hard to comprehend everything. But the tools and strategies you both gave us have been invaluable. We're beginning to see how this can help us."

Dorian nodded in agreement, squeezing Elaine's hand. "It's a challenge, but it's also a relief. Addressing the issue instead of tiptoeing around it... It feels like a weight has been lifted."

Vincent nodded, a proud smile spreading across his face. "That's the power of proactive communication," he said. "It allows you to tackle issues head-on, work through them, and prevent them from becoming long-standing conflicts. And, as you've seen, it can be incredibly cathartic."

Valerie, leaning forward, added, "And it's important to remember that having these proactive communication sessions shouldn't be just a one-off thing. It's a habit you both should cultivate and maintain.

It's about dedicating a few times each year to these intensive discussions. Focusing on areas of your relationship that might require strengthening or potential issues that could cause future disagreements."

"Can I add something?" Vincent asked, and upon receiving affirmative nods from the couple, he continued, "It's essential to approach these discussions prayerfully. Seek God's guidance before diving into these conversations. This can help you prepare to listen, speak, and engage without conflict.

The couple exchanged glances; their expressions reflected the new understanding they were gaining.

"Each hour you spend having a constructive dialogue about a challenging issue can lead to a year of peace by preventing an ongoing conflict over the same issue.

REBUILDING EMOTIONAL BRIDGES

"And remember," Vincent said, concluding the recap, "each hour you spend having a constructive dialogue about a challenging issue can lead to a year of peace by preventing an ongoing conflict over the same issue. It's worth considering - what sounds better: 1 day of Proactive Communication or 1 year of a mediocre marriage?"

It was as if their words lingered, heavy but hopeful. Elaine and Dorian locked eyes, their expressions determined. They had chosen to tackle their issues head-on and invest in proactive communication. It wouldn't be easy, but they knew it would be worth it. They had chosen a stronger, healthier, and happier marriage.

"Today," Valerie began, her tone serious yet empathetic, "we're delving into the heart of a successful marriage: emotional connection. This mandate is straightforward but perhaps one of the most crucial elements of a strong and enduring marriage."

Vincent picked up from where Valerie left off, "Always make a genuine effort to connect with your spouse emotionally. We cannot stress this enough. No matter the external circumstances, you must create a strong emotional bond with your spouse. This bond will serve as your fortress during stormy times."

There was a silence as Elaine and Dorian absorbed the weight of the mandate. Despite the words' simplicity, the task's gravity was still on them.

Elaine broke the silence, her voice teetering between hope and apprehension. "How do we do that? How do we connect emotionally, genuinely?"

Vincent nodded thoughtfully before speaking. "That's an important question, Elaine. Part of strengthening your emotional connection involves overcoming the obstacles that hinder it. One significant challenge is how conflict is handled. Unfortunately, the enemy, Satan, often uses conflict to disrupt the connection between spouses."

Valerie added, "That's right. He can twist communication – which should strengthen your bond – into a weapon to attack each other. That's why understanding and practicing certain rules during conflicts is crucial."

Vincent continued, "Let's discuss the 3 Rules to stop attacking each other and start drawing closer. These rules are essential in maintaining a healthy, God-centered relationship."

Rule #1: Talk Without Being Offensive

"Firstly, avoid name-calling or insulting each other. Reflect on the impact of your words before you speak. Choose words that build understanding and healing. Remember, self-control is key in using words that nurture, not hurt."

Rule #2: Listen Without Being Defensive

"Secondly, focus on truly understanding your spouse. Avoid getting defensive, as this often leads to tuning out what the other person is saying. Don't interrupt or shut down. Strive to comprehend their perspective before you respond. This requires patience and empathy."

Rule #3: Always Leave Your Spouse with Their Dignity

"Finally, don't aim to 'win' the argument. Focus on finding a solution that benefits both of you. Always address the issue at hand, not the person. Your words should reflect respect and uphold your spouse's dignity."

Valerie concluded, "By applying these rules, you can foster

love, respect, and understanding, even in disagreements. With God's guidance, these can become the foundation of your interactions, transforming conflict into a pathway for deeper connection."

Elaine and Dorian absorbed this new framework, understanding the profound impact these rules could have on their relationship.

Vincent and Valerie exchanged a look before she answered, "It also involves understanding each other's emotional needs and learning how to meet them.

Are they feeling anxious? Offer comfort. Are they feeling overjoyed? Share in their excitement. It's about being present in the emotional highs and lows of each other's lives."

"Open communication also plays a big role here," Vincent added. "You both need to be comfortable sharing your feelings, whether they are positive or negative. The process may initially seem uncomfortable if you are not accustomed to being emotionally expressive. But remember, vulnerability breeds connection."

Elaine and Dorian nodded, their faces reflecting a shared understanding. Valerie nodded in agreement as Vincent continued. "Connection is that intimate feeling of closeness with your spouse. It comes from spending quality time together, sharing experiences, and cherishing the moments you spend in each other's company. This connection lays the groundwork for effective communication." Valerie added,

"You can say and do all the "right" things, but if your spouse doesn't feel seen, heard, or understood, all that effort can be in vain. Love should be given, received, and reciprocated in a kind, reassuring way, especially in times of difficulty or disagreement."

"You see, communication involves exchanging information for understanding, but the connection between a husband and wife brings the true meaning and depth to it. The bond between you two is crucial, and we must always strive to maintain and deepen it."

"Genesis 2:22-23 in the Bible illustrates this concept beautifully," Vincent replied, "' Then the Lord God made a woman from the rib he had taken out of the man, and he brought her to the man. The man said, "This is now bone of my bones and flesh of my flesh; she shall be called 'woman,' for she was taken out of man."' This verse speaks of a husband and wife's inseparable bond and connection."

Vincent paused momentarily before adding, "I don't want to claim that men can even comprehend what it feels like to give birth or even know what giving birth feels like. However, this phrase 'bone of my bones and flesh of my flesh' signifies to us husbands that our wives are as close to us as someone we gave birth to. Therefore, we should care for her feelings, emotions, safety, and well-being just as we would our own."

This added perspective emphasizes the profound emotional and spiritual closeness that should exist between a husband and wife.

REESTABLISHING THEIR BOND

Building on that foundation, Valerie spoke up. "In the context of Marriage Mandate #4: Connection, let's consider the words from Matthew 19:6,

'So then, they are no longer two but one flesh. Therefore, what God has joined together, let not man separate.'

The term 'joined' here suggests clinging, cleaving to, staying with, and pursuing closely. It emphasizes that connection precedes communication.

We must realize that the phrase 'let not man separate' doesn't just mean outside influences, but can also mean...you. We can separate from each other by not seeking or pursuing ways to connect and reconnect."

Vincent agreed, "Exactly. A good connection establishes the basis for effective communication. You know the saying, 'People don't care how much you know until they know how much you care'? In marriage, saying and doing all the right things won't bridge the gap unless your spouse feels seen, heard, and understood."

Valerie continued, "We can see from 1 Corinthians 13:4-7 that love is more than an emotion; it's an action.

Love is patient, kind, not envious, boastful, arrogant, rude, self-seeking, or irritable, and doesn't record wrongs. Love is what fosters connection."

"Connection precedes communication."

INTIMACY BEYOND PHYSICAL CONNECTION

"And let's not forget the gift of sexual intimacy," Vincent added. "It was created by God to be enjoyed, and we believe that true sexual intimacy includes giving and receiving pleasure. There are generally three ways couples experience intimacy: some enjoy making love and want more of it; some want to but can't; and sometimes, there's no desire from either or both parties."

Vincent continued, "If you're a couple that enjoys lovemaking and wants more of it, that's wonderful. Continue enjoying and exploring each other, and look for ways to keep improving this level of intimacy.

"The greatest experience of sexual pleasure in marriage comes from pleasing your spouse."

Suppose you're a couple that wants to be intimate but can't; don't hesitate to discuss what might be hindering you. The barriers could be stress-related, physical, or biological.

Don't shy away from discussing it openly—sometimes, the solution can be as simple as getting more rest or a prescription from your physician.

And for those experiencing a lack of desire from one or both parties, we highly recommend seeing a therapist or counselor to address any underlying issues affecting you or your spouse."

"Love-making should not be used ONLY as a reward and NEVER as a punishment."

Valerie said, "Lovemaking should not be used ONLY as a reward and NEVER as a punishment. It should be a mutual exchange, expressed with tenderness, intensity, respect, and frequency."

"Elaine and Dorian exchanged glances as Vincent continued, "So, how can you foster this connection and continue to reconnect over time? Here are a few practical tips."

Valerie spoke, "When talking about connection, think of it in five dimensions: Spiritually, Physically, Intellectually, Recreationally, and Emotionally—**SPIRE** for short.

Spiritually, you can bond through shared moments in prayer, worship, or doing a Bible plan together.

Physically, intimacy isn't just about sex; it's also about touch, hugs, and simple gestures that make you feel close.

Intellectually, make time to discuss daily topics of interest and your views on deeper issues.

Recreationally, find activities you both enjoy—whether it's puzzles, movies, or going on hikes.

And **emotionally**, be ready to share your vulnerabilities, successes, and dreams."

"The body will follow the part of you that you feed the most."

Vincent nodded in agreement and added, "Another handy acronym to remember how to enhance these connections is **P.L.U.S**. First, **Plan** quality time together.

Carve out moments where you can focus on each other, away from the distractions of everyday life. Second, **Listen** to each other's hopes, dreams, and goals. Truly hearing your spouse fosters emotional closeness.

Third, **Uplift** one another during the trials and tribulations that inevitably arise in life. Lastly, **Spend time** in the Word of God together; it can serve as a solid foundation for your relationship."

"With that," Vincent and Valerie smiled warmly at Elaine and Dorian. The room became peaceful as Elaine and Dorian quietly digested the wealth of understanding they'd just unearthed. As Elaine turned her gaze towards Dorian, her fingers weaving through his, she was eager to embark on this journey deeper into their emotional connection."

THE RECONNECTION

The evening air filled the room, carrying with it the promise of renewal as Elaine and Dorian returned home. They sat on their shared bed. The atmosphere was tinged with a new sense of awareness and intimacy. Soft jazz music floated from a speaker on the nightstand, its melodies intertwining with the complexities of their emotions.

Elaine looked at Dorian, her eyes searching for the man she married, whose love had once been her sanctuary. "Dorian, do you remember when we first met? How could we talk for hours and feel like every moment was precious?"

Dorian's gaze met hers. "I do. And," he hesitated, choosing his words carefully, "I've missed that."

A smile tugged at the corners of Dorian's mouth as a memory surfaced. "Remember how your dad used to fuss at you for being on the phone all night with me? He always said we were the reason for the high phone bill."

Elaine chuckled, the sound bubbling up from a well of shared memories. "He was probably right," she said, her eyes sparkling with amusement.

"He was probably right," Dorian echoed, and they both let out a genuine, hearty laugh, the kind that comes from a place of deep connection and shared history.

Elaine felt her eyes brim with tears, tears of joy. She wanted to articulate the yearning that had been dormant for so long, a desire not just for the physical but for the emotional and spiritual connection they once shared. But words seemed too trivial, too inadequate for the enormity of her emotions. She opened her mouth, but no words came.

Understanding filled Dorian's eyes as he drew closer, gently taking her face. "You don't have to say it, Elaine. I've missed it too. I've missed us."

With those words, a connection was rekindled— a spark reignited. They knew what the other was thinking and, in unison, moved closer, sealing their newfound understanding with a heartfelt kiss. As they held each other, every touch and every look seemed to bridge the gap that had formed between them over the years.

Their lovemaking was a rediscovery, a passionate dance that honored both their history and the fresh start they were giving themselves. For the first time in a long time, they felt like they were one— emotionally, spiritually, and physically.

Afterward, they lay in each other's arms, the soft hum of the night filling the room around them. "How have we been depriving ourselves of this? This connection?" Dorian wondered aloud.

Elaine looked into his eyes, her gaze filled with a sense of belonging. It doesn't matter now, but what matters is that we've found it again, and we won't let go." Then, a funny thing happened. For hours, they talked as if every moment was precious."

As it dawned, everything became clear. The two knew this was not the end but the beginning of a journey of reconnection.

THE REFLECTION

In the days to follow, Elaine found herself flipping through an old photo album under the soft glow of the living room, her eyes tracing the lines of a younger Dorian, radiant and unburdened. It had been a while since he'd confessed his addiction, and she insisted he seek help.

There was a budding hope in her heart in those initial days, nurtured by Dorian's commitment to addiction recovery and marriage counseling. As time went on, she began noticing positive changes in him.

She was tired—no, exhausted—of fighting in her marriage. It was time to fight for it instead.

But even with these small steps forward, Elaine felt something was still amiss. As she poured over the old photographs, she felt a lump in her throat. "Can we do this?" Elaine wondered. The tender moments and new-found connection they'd discovered were being overshadowed. Elaine realized that the enemy—Satan himself—was trying to gain a foothold in their marriage by using fear to discourage her. Her heart ached at the notion that dark forces could be reveling in their struggles. But instead of sinking deeper into despair, she felt a flicker of resolve.

She was tired—no, exhausted—of fighting in her marriage. It was time to fight for it instead. To do that, she needed to arm herself with prayer, love, and open communication, using the truths that Vincent and Valerie had shared as her weapons. There was no room for complacency when their future was at stake.

Elaine let her fingers rest on the closed album, grounding herself in the promise of better days. A spark of determination ignited within her as she resolved to take action, not to let the enemy have the last laugh.

As she put the album away, Elaine took a deep breath, acknowledging the lingering fear but choosing to push it aside. She resolved to speak with Dorian when he returned from his meeting, believing that open hearts and candid conversations were the way forward. The tension in their relationship was undeniable, but Elaine's hope, faith, and trust were stronger. She was certain that Dorian felt the same strain. After all, it takes two to tango, and they were both ready to find their rhythm again!

THE CONNECTION MANDATE:

I acknowledge and accept the necessity of authentic, intimate, and emotional connection in marriage. It must be coupled with communication to render it effective.

Study Guide

next page ☞

Study Guide
Marriage Mandate #4: *Connection*

Chapter Summary:
The fourth marriage mandate delves into the essence of emotional and spiritual connectivity. This chapter highlights the importance of building and maintaining a deeply intimate bond between spouses. Spiritual, physical, intellectual, recreational, and emotional connectivity are essential to maintaining a resilient and fulfilling marriage.

Key Concepts and Takeaways:

- **Spiritual Bonding:** Engage in shared faith activities and spiritual practices to deepen your marital bond.

- **Physical Intimacy Beyond Sex:** Prioritize both sexual and non-sexual physical affection to nurture your connection.

- **Intellectual Compatibility:** Engage in stimulating conversations and explore mutual intellectual interests to strengthen your bond.

- **Emotional Intimacy:** Work on understanding each other's emotions, empathizing deeply, and openly sharing feelings to build emotional closeness in your relationship.

Discussion Questions:

1. How can a marriage develop a deeper emotional connection?
  - Give examples in the story of how their manner of verbal or nonverbal communication negatively affected their connection.

2. In what ways do you express physical affection apart from sexual intimacy?
  - Physical affection acts do not always lead to romantic interaction, but they are vital components of emotional and relational intimacy in a relationship.

3. Do you and your spouse enjoy recreational activities together?
  - Explore new hobbies or activities to strengthen your bond with your spouse.

4. How do you maintain emotional intimacy in your relationship?
  - Discuss ways you share your feelings, support each other emotionally, and empathize.

5. Can you think of a time when you felt particularly connected to your spouse? What made it special?
  - Find out what makes your spouse feel more connected to you.

6. What steps can you take to strengthen an area of connection that may be lacking?
  - Remember that what your spouse needs to feel connected to you may differ from you.

THE CONNECTION ACTION PLAN:
How do we improve your connection?

- **Plan activities you both enjoy.** Discover new hobbies and interests. Be open to exploring one another's interests from time to time. (walk, read, watch a movie, play a game, go to sporting events, plan trips...)

- **Share your hopes and dreams.** Set goals and strategies to reach them. This is a great way to connect on a deeper level. Create individual and collective vision boards.

- **Support one another emotionally and physically.** Be there for each other both emotionally and physically, staying attentive and accessible during both joyful and challenging moments in your relationship.

- **Spend quality time together.** Eliminate distractions, such as phones and interruptions, and fully engage with each other to be truly present in the moment.

- **Mentorship:** Connect with a couple who mirrors Covenant Marriage. They can offer valuable insights, advice, and perspectives based on their experiences.

- **Re-read the Marriage Mandate on Connection:** What does this mandate mean to you?

Weekly Prayer:

Dear Lord,

In our journey to strengthen the connection within our marriage, we humbly seek Your guidance and support. Inspire us to engage in activities that bring us closer, discover new interests, and share in each other's passions. Grant us the wisdom to openly share our hopes, dreams, and goals, fostering a deeper understanding and bond between us. Help us be emotionally and physically present for one another in joyous and challenging times. Bless our time together, allowing us to focus wholly on one another, free from distractions. And lead us to mentors who exemplify Your love in their marriages so we may learn and grow independently. May our connection reflect Your love and grace, growing us stronger each day.

In Jesus' name, Amen.

Reflection Notes:

This is why a man leaves his father and
mother and bonds with his wife, and they
become one flesh. ***Both the man and his wife
were naked, yet felt no shame.***

Genesis 2:24-25

Marriage Mandate #5: *Calibration*

"Both the man and his wife were naked, yet felt no shame."

EMBRACING CHANGE

Meanwhile, Dorian found himself navigating the winding road back from his addiction counselor's office, a torrent of conflicting emotions threatening to pull him off course. The meeting had brought forth probing questions, like a beam of light piercing through his carefully constructed defenses. Why did he want to beat his addiction? Was it for Elaine? His career? The possibility of a family? Or was it for himself?

He gripped the steering wheel tighter, the cool leather offering little comfort. He didn't know the answers. He didn't want Elaine to leave him, but part of him wondered if she might be happier without him. He questioned if he could ever become the man Elaine deserved, the man she had once fallen in love with. The thought of losing another child haunted him. It clung to him like a shadow, casting a dark cloud over their dreams of starting a family.

As Dorian drove, his thoughts raced, each one vying for attention. His fears and doubts bore down on him like the world had taken residence on his shoulders. How could he possibly voice his apprehensions to Elaine? The acceleration of his heart echoed the escalating speed of his car. His vision blurred as the lines on the road seemed to melt into each other, the onslaught of tears transforming clarity into chaos.

The potential loss of his family was unbearable. In a moment of raw despair, he screamed to God, his voice filling the car, echoing his tumultuous emotions. He pulled over to the side of the road, his body trembling as he took a deep breath. He closed his eyes and prayed, his words simple and sincere. He asked God for help, strength to overcome his addiction, and to become the husband Elaine deserved.

His heart poured out with his prayer; his burdens laid bare. But as he surrendered his struggles, he felt an unexpected relief. It was as if a ray of hope had pierced through the storm clouds, offering him a glimpse of a clearer sky.

He remembered he wasn't alone. He had Vincent and Valerie, their teachings acting as beacons guiding him through the darkest corners of his journey. And he had Elaine, his steadfast rock, who remained by his side despite his shortcomings and the emotional distance he had created after the loss of their child.

Dorian chuckled softly. Amid the storm that was their life, he realized God had sent them Vincent and Valerie. They were their spotters, helping them lift the weight of their struggles. Despite their burdens, Dorian was reminded they weren't carrying them alone. As he resumed his drive, a newfound sense of determination and hope replaced the earlier despair. For the first time in a long time, Dorian felt the possibility of a better future for himself and their marriage.

THE TALK

As Dorian's car approached the driveway, the sound permeated the walls of their home, reaching Elaine. It acted as a drumroll, ramping up the air's tension. Their hearts raced in their chests, mirroring the other's anxious anticipation. The impending conversation hung over them like a storm cloud, and both wondered how it would unfold.

The car door closing reached Elaine's ears, followed by the familiar keys jingling. As Dorian turned the doorknob, Elaine watched from the hallway, second-guessing her decision. She pondered if now was the right time to open up this conversation. Should they wait until their next meeting with Vincent and Valerie? At the same time, Dorian, on the other side of the door, was wrestling with similar doubts.

As the door swung open, they greeted each other, their smiles acting as masks hiding the turmoil beneath. Their eyes met, each looking for answers in the other. Words hovered on their lips, the same words that most couples dread to utter. In the heavy silence, they both spoke up at the same time, their voices intermingling.

"We need to talk."

Their simultaneous utterance took them both by surprise. They stared at each other, the shared admission hanging between them. It was a moment that validated their connection and reaffirmed that they were both on the same page, each aware of the other's worries and ready to confront them. Despite the apprehension, they also felt an undercurrent of relief — an unspoken agreement that, regardless of the challenges, they would face them together. The difficult conversation they had been avoiding was about to begin, but they would tackle it hand in hand this time.

SOMETHING'S DIFFERENT

After their simultaneous admissions, Elaine and Dorian found themselves in startled silence. Dorian, yearning to break the ice, deferred to Elaine, gesturing for her to go first. But then, they did it again. Like a strange echo, "you first" spilled from their lips simultaneously. With a courteous nod and a wry smile, Dorian gestured to Elaine, silently insisting she lead the conversation.

Elaine took a moment, gathering her thoughts. She knew they couldn't progress without acknowledging the growing chasm between them, the unseen weight of Dorian's increasing distance. Her mind raced as she sought the right words and the appropriate tone to address the looming issue.

However, as she was about to begin, she paused. There was something different about Dorian tonight. A softness in his eyes that she hadn't seen in what felt like forever. His eyelids still bore the telltale signs of recent tears - slightly puffy and red. Yet, the glimmer in his eyes wasn't borne of tears. It originated somewhere deep within him.

Curiosity took hold of her. She felt an unexpected hope,

and her worries about initiating the conversation faded into the background. She gestured back towards Dorian, encouragingly smiled, and indicated he should start.

THE APOLOGY

Dorian opened his mouth to speak, struggling to suppress the surge of emotions threatening to overwhelm him. His words caught in his throat as tears started trickling down his face. He apologized for his increasing distance for failing to support Elaine fully in their shared grief over losing their child. As his tears flowed freely, he expressed remorse for his addiction, lying about using her credentials and not being honest about his struggles.

Sitting down, Dorian let himself fully experience the despair as he described the excruciating pain he'd hidden after learning he wouldn't become a father. He regretted leaving Elaine to face it seemingly alone, believing he was protecting her by hiding his pain. He realized now how that had only compounded her suffering.

With a trembling voice, he admitted understanding the true meaning of their marriage. He recognized their spiritual covenant with each other and God and how they were never meant to face marriage alone. God was there, ready to help if they only included Him in their daily lives. He acknowledged the importance of their vow to stand together "for better or for worse" and how much they needed each other in these challenging times.

Dorian admitted that blocking communication only made matters worse. He now understood how vital it was to maintain their connection. Firmly grasping Elaine's hands, he vowed to promise to do everything in his power to be the best man and husband he could be. He also acknowledged that he could only do this with God's help. Then he embraced Elaine and planted on her lips the most passionate kiss they'd ever shared in a long time.

After breaking the kiss, Dorian took a moment to catch his breath and asked Elaine what she wanted to say. Taking in the man before her, Elaine paused for a moment. Her prayer had been answered. Looking deeply into Dorian's eyes, the only response she could think of was, "Ditto."

Dorian looked at Elaine with a sense of determination in her eyes and said those words Elaine was so blessed to hear, "Let's pray together."

EMBRACING A NEW CHAPTER

It had been about a month and a half since Dorian and Elaine's last session with Vincent and Valerie.

Life, as it tends to do, had become busier for both of them, throwing them curveballs that they had to navigate. Elaine's work at the hospital had been more demanding than usual, with a shortage of staff leading to longer hours and a need for her expertise with various patients.

Meanwhile, Dorian started his new architectural firm, and his skills and creativity were more sought after than ever before. Their regular sessions with Vincent and Valerie had been temporarily paused due to the daily hustle and bustle. Still, it had not stopped their progress or commitment to improving their relationship. They were still doing their homework and looking forward to it together.

Despite the delay, the two couples found a common time in their busy schedules to reconvene. Elaine and Dorian were dedicated to pressing forward, a testament to their commitment to their relationship. They understood the significance of what they were doing - reshaping and reinforcing their relationship with their love and respect for each other.

The room was warm as the two couples sat down, the energy and atmosphere noticeably different from their previous sessions. Vincent and Valerie observed Dorian and Elaine with a smile. Their interactions, smiles, and slight lingering touches suggested the couple had experienced a breakthrough.

"Well, it seems like things have progressed quite significantly," Vincent said, starting the session with a tone of positivity. He and Valerie exchanged a glance before she added, "We can sense a change in your connection, and it's quite remarkable."

Dorian and Elaine shared a knowing look before Dorian turned back to Vincent and Valerie, nodding.

"We've made some progress," he admitted, wrapping an arm around Elaine. Elaine leaned into Dorian's side, her smile saying more than words could.

"That's excellent news. We've come a long way in our journey, and it's good to see that you're moving in the right direction. Now, let's discuss the final chapter - Calibration and Recalibration in Marriage," Vincent began.

EXPECTATIONS

"The first step in calibration is setting expectations. Realize that the idea that everything falls perfectly into place once we fall in love and get married is not often the case. It's a beautiful thought, but the reality is seldom so straightforward," Valerie continued.

Vincent said, "Taking the time to acknowledge and address issues head-on shows strength, commitment, and dedication to the relationship. It's important to remember that it only takes one person to start the process, even if initially, only one spouse wants to work on the marriage."

"Setting boundaries isn't about controlling one another, but creating a respectful environment."

ESTABLISHING BOUNDARIES

"Setting expectations also involves establishing boundaries. Setting boundaries isn't about controlling one another, but creating a respectful environment where you both feel secure and loved," Vincent explained.

"For instance," Valerie added, "you might decide to always speak to one another with mutual respect, never go to bed angry, and not allow any abuse - be it physical, mental, verbal, or financial. Maybe you'll decide not to spend above an agreed-upon amount without consulting one another or to listen without interruption, verbally and non-verbally."

REALISTIC REALIZATIONS

"And throughout this calibration process," Vincent continued, "you need realistic realizations. Calibration is not a one-time process, and it's ongoing. It's normal for adjustments to be needed over time as you both grow and evolve. It's about creating a harmonious balance that benefits both of you."

"Remember," Valerie concluded, "Calibration and recalibration deepen the trust between spouses, providing a 'home base' for the couple to return to in times of struggle. It also protects the relationship from negative influences, promoting greater intimacy and vulnerability."

With that, the room fell silent as Dorian and Elaine pondered over the information shared, their hands intertwined, ready to face whatever came their way together.

The focus becomes doing what is right for the relationship, rather than determining who is right."

CALIBRATION IN MARRIAGE

The session resumed after a short break, and Vincent and Valerie shared a look before continuing. Vincent cleared his throat, catching Dorian and Elaine's attention. "Now we move on to the concept of 'Center of Spec' in the context of marriage."

Valerie explained, "In technical terms, calibration compares a measurement instrument or system and a known standard. In our case, that standard is the Biblical teachings on marriage. The 'Center of Spec' is the ideal point that everything is calibrated towards."

Vincent then expanded, "The tools we use to calibrate our relationship are God's truth and wisdom. When husband and wife agree to rely on these, selfish motives, attitudes, and actions are diminished. The focus becomes doing what is right for the relationship, rather than determining who is right."

"A marriage needs periodic adjustments and maintenance like any system."

"Calibration and recalibration in marriage, as we've previously touched upon, establish expectations, create a baseline for conflict resolution, protect the relationship from negative influences, and promote intimacy and trust," Valerie reemphasized.

"Yet, it's also crucial to note that effective recalibration requires creating a safe space for open, honest discussions," Vincent added, highlighting the importance of communication.

ROLES AND RESPONSIBILITIES

"Here's where we often find a lot of confusion, especially concerning roles in a marriage," Valerie pointed out. "The concept of a man being the 'head' in a marriage doesn't mean he is superior. Instead, it signifies different roles and responsibilities. God holds him accountable."

Vincent continued, "Similarly, women hold equal worth and value. Their role in decision-making and providing counsel to their husbands is vital. A wife being a 'helper' represents God's intervention.

In Genesis 2:18, God promises to make a helper for the first man. The Hebrew word for "helper" is Ezer (pronounced

122

like "ay-zer)." The word is used 66 times in the Bible to describe God's strength, protection, power, help, and ability to rescue. As a result, God has inserted his super with our natural, making the wife a 'super helper' in marriage.

> *"Effective recalibration requires creating a safe space for open, honest discussions."*

SETTING EXPECTATIONS

"But how does one recalibrate in a marriage?" Valerie asked, looking between Dorian and Elaine. "You start by establishing standards of expectations and boundaries. Acknowledge your imperfections and learn to forgive. And when conflict arises, resolve it in a manner beneficial to both of you."

"It's crucial to discern when it is God speaking and when it's your emotions, especially when making significant decisions about your relationship. Your 'Center of Spec' is that solid reference point that helps you realign whenever your marriage encounters variations," Vincent added.

"The goal," Valerie concluded, "is to keep recalibrating your marriage based on your 'Center of Spec,' ensuring it aligns with God's plan and purpose for marriage as outlined in the scriptures."

After a few minutes, Vincent concluded by saying, "It is

important to remember to serve your spouse by meeting their needs, by understanding their basic needs, as we discussed previously, not just what you want." Like a waiter taking your order, it's about meeting their needs, not dictating them."

"Serve your spouse by meeting their needs, not dictating them."

Together, they led Dorian and Elaine in this confession:

"I accept and acknowledge that my spouse and I are responsible for setting healthy boundaries in our relationship. We must honor one another and agree to recalibrate whenever necessary."

The room held a warm, heartfelt atmosphere as Vincent and Valerie shared their pride. They commended Dorian and Elaine on their immense progress, knowing the process took work.

"Nothing worth having or saving rarely is," Valerie reminded them, her eyes filled with admiration for the couple. Vincent nodded in agreement, echoing her sentiments.

They invited the couple to share their most significant takeaways from all the sessions.

Dorian cleared his throat, glancing at Elaine before speaking. "The first mandate, Covenant, made us realize that marriage isn't just an agreement; it's a sacred promise.

That understanding helped us see our relationship in a whole new light."

Elaine took over, her eyes shining with a newfound understanding. "Commitment taught us the true essence of dedication, that it's not just about saying 'I do,' but standing by that promise every day."

"Communication was another key takeaway," Dorian continued, his voice carrying newfound conviction. "We learned that having proactive, personal, and intimate communication with each other would help us understand each other better, preventing miscommunication."

"And then, Connection. It taught us the importance of sharing experiences and creating memories together," Elaine added, her hand finding Dorian's fingers interlocking naturally.

"Finally," Dorian concluded, "Calibration and Recalibration. These mandates showed us that a marriage needs periodic adjustments and maintenance like any system. It isn't something that just runs on its own. We must keep calibrating our relationship to align with our 'Center of Spec.'"

The couple then shared a knowing look, a mysterious glint in their eyes that piqued Vincent and Valerie's curiosity. "What is it?" Valerie asked, noticing their secretive smiles.

With their hands clasped tightly together, Dorian and Elaine looked at each other before turning to Vincent and Valerie. In unison, they declared, "We're pregnant."

The room erupted with joy. Vincent and Valerie leaped from their seats, and the space was immediately filled with laughter, excited cheers, and warm congratulations. They embraced Dorian and Elaine, the joy in the room palpable. It was the perfect culmination of their journey together - the beginning of a new chapter filled with hope, love, and a deepened understanding of marriage.

THE CALIBRATION MANDATE:

I accept and acknowledge that my spouse and I are responsible for setting healthy boundaries in our relationship. We must honor one another and agree to calibrate and re-calibrate whenever necessary.

Study Guide
next page ☞

THE 5 Marriage Mandates

Covenant · Commitment · Communication · Connection · Calibration

Study Guide

Study Guide
Marriage Mandate #5: *Calibration*

Chapter Summary:

Calibration centers on establishing and upholding boundaries to safeguard the quality and longevity of a successful marriage. It involves implementing shared values and goals that enable the couple to achieve the agreed-upon physical, emotional, and spiritual standard of living, rooted in biblical principles and tailored to their family's needs. Calibration also considers the necessity of adapting to the inevitable changes that life may bring.

Key Concepts and Takeaways:

- **Be willing to adjust:** Marriage demands continuous effort and recalibration to adjust to life's challenges and each other's evolving needs.

- **Set Clear Expectations:** Place importance on establishing transparent and realistic expectations of one another.

- **Define Boundaries:** Acknowledge the vital role of boundaries in preserving respect, understanding, and expectation within the relationship.

- **Embrace Adaptation and Growth:** Understand and welcome the necessity for both personal and mutual growth within the marriage.

Discussion Questions:

1. How is the need for calibration or re-calibration demonstrated in Elaine and Dorian's marriage regarding his journey through addiction recovery?
- Life can present unforeseen challenges that require adaptation to preserve the health and integrity of the marriage relationship.

2. Can you identify any boundaries that have been important in your relationship that have been tested?
- Discuss the reason for these boundaries and how they have helped sustain your relationship.

3. What growth or changes have you observed in your spouse and yourself since marriage?
- Share your observations on personal and relational growth.

4. Are there areas in your marriage that currently need recalibration?
- Identify how you and your spouse can agree upon the necessary changes.

5. How can you meet one another's needs as you grow and change over time?
- Discuss ways to stay attuned to each other's evolving needs while agreeing to prioritize both your own health and wellness and your marriage.

THE CALIBRATION ACTION PLAN:
What can we do to re-calibrate our relationship?

- **Establish a standard.** What boundaries and expectations do each of you have for your relationship? Are they cohesive? Once you know what you both expect, you can start to work on meeting those expectations.

- **Acknowledge your imperfections.** No one is perfect, including you and your spouse. It's important to acknowledge your imperfections and to be willing to forgive your spouse for theirs.

- **Plan Ahead:** Identify potential challenges and discuss strategies to address them together.

- **Re-read the Marriage Mandate on *Calibration*:** What does this mandate mean to you?

Weekly Prayer:

Heavenly Father,

We seek Your wisdom and grace as we learn to calibrate and recalibrate our marriage. Guide us to establish clear expectations and boundaries that honor You and each other. Help us to acknowledge and accept our imperfections, fostering a spirit of forgiveness and understanding. As we establish a plan, grant us the insight to foresee potential challenges and the strength to address them together. May our marriage be a testament to Your love and faithfulness. Strengthen our bond, Lord, as we align our relationship with Your purpose.

In Jesus' name, we pray, Amen.

Reflection Notes:

Last Chapter: *The Follow-up*

WHEN ONE JOURNEY ENDS, A NEW ONE BEGINS

It was an especially vibrant sunny afternoon as Vincent and Valerie drove through the quiet streets. Their destination? The home of Dorian and Elaine. Today marked a special occasion - Dorian and Elaine had invited them to a baby shower, a celebration of new beginnings.

The drive was a trip down memory lane. They recalled Dorian and Elaine's initial visits, which were filled with tension and uncertainty. Yet, over time, a profound bond of love and understanding had blossomed between them. "Their transformation has been remarkable," Vincent remarked, admiration evident in his eyes. With a gentle smile, Valerie responded, "Indeed, witnessing their journey has been a blessing."

They reflected on how their past wasn't much different from Dorian and Elaine's. Vincent and Valerie, too, faced challenges in their marriage, but they conquered each one, fortified by love and faith. "We've walked the same path," It had been over a decade since they, too, stood on the cliff edge of separation, their marriage threatened by the same pitfalls they now helped other couples navigate.

They glanced at one another, knowing what the other was thinking. The sentiment was conveyed without a word. A sweet silence filled the car as they lost themselves in thought, reminiscing about Dorian and Elaine and their journey.

They savored this quiet moment, hearts filled with gratitude for the love they had rekindled and the opportunity to guide other couples in their journey. They were living proof of the transformative power of love, dedication, and faith.

CELEBRATING NEW BEGINNINGS

Arriving at Dorian and Elaine's home, they were greeted with laughter and chatter, the air buzzing with excitement and joy. The house was architecturally stunning and beautifully decorated. Dorian must have designed this house, Vincent said to Valerie, and Valerie nodded in agreement, saying Elaine probably decorated it. Loved ones gathered around, eagerly anticipating the newest family member's arrival.

THE WELCOMING

To their surprise, the special guest was already there.

Dorian and Elaine had welcomed their baby into the world. With gentle excitement, they handed the newborn to Vincent and Valerie.

As they cradled the infant, a surge of emotion washed over them. Vincent spoke, "This beautiful baby symbolizes the new life and the rebirth of your love and relationship, and we are so blessed to witness your new beginning."

At Vincent's words, Elaine and Dorian exchanged a

knowing look, their eyes sparkling with a shared secret. They couldn't help but be tickled by Vincent's choice of words - "new beginning."

With a mixture of excitement and emotion, Elaine turned to Vincent and Valerie, her voice filled with joy. "You know, it's funny you should say 'new beginning,'" she began, her gaze shifting to the tiny bundle in their arms. "We haven't shared our baby's name yet because we wanted this moment to be special."

Dorian, his eyes brimming with pride and happiness, as Elaine continued, "We thought long and hard about how to honor this incredible journey we've been on, the struggles we've overcome, and the fresh start we've been given. And then it struck us."

Elaine gently took the baby from Vincent and said warmly, "There was no better way to honor our new beginning than to name our baby... Genesis."

Vincent and Valerie couldn't help but feel proud and humbled to have been part of Dorian and Elaine's journey toward understanding, acceptance, and rekindled love.

This was more than just a follow-up visit; it was a celebration. They were filled with emotion as this was a reminder of the countless couples they had helped throughout the years and the lives they had touched.

Having been prophesied about them 20+ years ago, they were on their way to becoming that "couple of example."

CELEBRATING THE PROMISE OF THE FUTURE

Vincent and Valerie remembered how God used their pain to push them into purpose. For as long as possible, they would dedicate themselves to restoring many marriages and families through the same hope, love, and faith that Dorian and Elaine had now realized.

This is why a man leaves his father and mother and bonds with his wife, and they become one flesh. Both the man and his wife were naked, yet felt no shame. - Genesis 2:24-25

About The Authors

Vincent and Valerie Woodard are the founders of Couples Pursuit. Vincent is an ordained minister and elder, certified in Marriage and Couples Therapy and Family Counseling, an entrepreneur, and a speaker.

Valerie is also an ordained elder with a bachelor's degree in theology and a master's in Christian Counseling. Valerie is an accomplished singer and songwriter. She is also an entrepreneur.

The Woodards have been married since May 27, 2000, and share two beautiful daughters, a son, a daughter-in-love, and one grandson.

They were married by their former pastor, who said during the ceremony that they would be a "couple of example." Initially, music was the path they assumed they might take because of their mutual love for creating music, but neither Vincent nor Valerie had any idea just what being a "couple of example" had in store.

Like most married couples, their journey has encompassed many trials and triumphs. Because of faith in God and His faithfulness to them, the Woodards have come through every challenge better, stronger, and more passionate than ever.

Fast forward 24+ years later, they are inspired and equipped to do so, and they are compelled to share their experience of being saved from the brink of divorce to help others. Through videos covering anything from courtship to covenant to commitment and Marriage Mentoring Sessions, Vincent and Valerie aspire to spread love, hope, and faith to couples worldwide.

It's common for couples to express the need to get away together or go to a retreat to fix or repair their relationship rather than dealing with the root issues causing problems today. The time has come for Total Surrender, No Retreat... It's time for Couples Pursuit.

To learn more, visit: couplespursuit.com

Need relationship advice? Book a call:
couplespursuit.com/talk

SOCIAL LINKS
Instagram:instagram.com/couplespursuit
Facebook: facebook.com/couplespursuit
Couples Pursuit Facebook group:
facebook.com/groups/couplespursuit

FREE MASTERCLASS on Effective Communication and all other links and resources can be found here:
couplespursuit.com/links

Notes:

MARRIAGE MANDATE #1: COVENANT

- **Genesis 2:24** - Discussed in the context of marriage as a sacred covenant.
- **Ephesians 5:25-26** - Mentioned when discussing the reflection of God's love in marriage.
- **Covenant** (biblical). (2023, December 9). In Wikipedia. https://en.wikipedia.org/wiki/Covenant_(biblical)

MARRIAGE MANDATE #2: COMMITMENT

- **National Institutes of Health study on divorce** - Referenced for statistics on commitment issues leading to divorce.
- **Malachi 2:13-14** - Used to emphasize the sanctity of marriage and God's view on how spouses should treat each other.

MARRIAGE MANDATE #3: COMMUNICATION

- **Ephesians 4:15** - Mentioned in the context of speaking the truth in love for healthy communication.
- **Hierarchy of Needs, Abraham Maslow** - The concept is adapted and backed by Biblical principles.
- **Isaiah 41:10** - Referenced for the importance of security in a relationship.
- **1 John 4:7-8** - Used to discuss the importance of love and belonging in marriage.
- **Philippians 2:3** - Referenced in the context of respect and recognition within marriage.

Mindfulness STOP Skill: DBT STOP Technique: Find Calm

Albert Bonfil

https://cogbtherapy.com/mindfulness-meditation-blog/mindfuln ess-stop-skill

MARRIAGE MANDATE #4: CONNECTION

- **Genesis 2:22-23** - Discussed to illustrate the bond and connection between a husband and wife.

- **Matthew 19:6** is used to emphasize the importance of connection in marriage.

- **1 Corinthians 13:4-7** - Mentioned in the context of the nature of love and its role in fostering connection.

MARRIAGE MANDATE #5: CALIBRATION

- **Ephesians 2:10** - Discussed finding purpose and recalibrating in marriage.

OTHER REFERENCES:

- Emerson Eggerichs's book, 'Love and Respect: The Love She Most Desires; The Respect He Desperately Needs' - Quoted in Chapter 2 in the context of commitment.

"The '3 Rules to stop attacking each other and start drawing closer' presented in Chapter 4 were adapted from a quote by Reverend Cecil 'Chip' Murray."

THE 5 Marriage Mandates

Made in the USA
Middletown, DE
01 September 2024

60301312R00080